THRIVING
in the
STORM

THRIVING
in the
STORM

Nine Principles to Help You Overcome Any Adversity

BILL MURPHY

Skyhorse Publishing

Skyhorse Publishing books may be purchased in bulk at special discounts for sales promotion, corporate gifts, fundraising, or educational purposes. Special editions can also be created to specifications. For details, contact the Special Sales Department, Skyhorse Publishing, 307 West 36th Street, 11th Floor, New York, NY 10018 or info@skyhorsepublishing.com.

Skyhorse® and Skyhorse Publishing® are registered trademarks of Skyhorse Publishing, Inc.®, a Delaware corporation.

Visit our website at www.skyhorsepublishing.com.

10 9 8 7 6 5 4 3 2 1

Library of Congress Cataloging-in-Publication Data is available on file.

Cover design by David Ter-Avanesyan

Print ISBN: 978-1-5107-7500-8
Ebook ISBN: 978-1-5107-7510-7

Printed in the United States of America

Contents

Introduction

Ever since I was a kid, anytime someone told me I couldn't do something, I wanted to prove them wrong, and that mentality has stuck with me my entire life. It's how I found myself in Florida in 2019 about to participate in my first Ironman.

Around 3,000 people showed up for the event. Typically, about 500 of those 3,000 either get a DNQ (did not qualify by finishing in under 17 hours) or DNF (did not finish). I had set a goal to finish the race in under 14 hours, but it was really all about finishing, period. I was not going to end up a DNQ or a DNF, but when I showed up for orientation, that's when the self-doubt started to creep in.

I had run the Boston Marathon four times, but the Ironman was a different beast—a 2.4-mile swim and 112 miles on the bike followed by a full 26.2-mile marathon at the end. When I started training six months earlier, I couldn't swim two laps in the pool without gasping for air, and almost fell over when trying to test ride a new bike. I had come a long way, but I still didn't feel like I belonged there. Everyone around me looked like professional athletes. They were talking about the mechanics of their bike, the gait of their stride, and the max heart rate they needed to be at during the race. I didn't know what the hell any of that meant. It was intimidating. I was never the biggest, fastest, or strongest. I always had to work harder than everyone else to earn my spot as a kid, and that never changed when I got older. Those are feelings we all experience, but what most people don't realize is that you can't wait for that feeling to go away before you get started. You just have to do it and will your way through with grit and determination, so that's what I did.

I'd love to say that I breezed through my first Ironman and blew away my target time because of my preparation, but that didn't happen. I was freezing when I got out of the water after the swim, I got two flat tires on the bike, and my legs were rubber when I started the marathon, but I remembered what my coach had told me. I trusted that my nutrition and training would pay off, and I crossed the finish line in 13 hours and 56 minutes—just under my 14-hour goal. That's when those feelings of doubt finally disappeared. Just like after every race, I finally felt like I belonged with this group of athletes.

I accomplished a lot in 2019. In addition to finishing my first Ironman, I earned my black belt in Krav Maga and completed my fourth Boston Marathon. Next, I was going to turn my attention to finishing the year as my company's number-one mortgage originator in sales. On the surface, life seemed great. I should have been on top of the world, and to an outsider, it looked like I had it made, but something was very, very wrong. It had been bubbling under the surface my entire life, and I was trying to run away from it, but wasn't able to run any longer.

I had read an ESPN article about NBA players discussing their childhood depression and how it was nothing to be ashamed of. Something about that article resonated with me. I was a guy who grew up thinking men didn't get depressed. That was for the weak. I called those guys soft because I thought that was something to be embarrassed about. But after reading that article, I cried. And I've only cried a handful of times in my life. I was starting to recognize the patterns in my own life. *Oh my God! Am I depressed? Is that what's happening to me?* I had to dive in and learn more.

I've always been a self-help junkie. I got my master's in psychology and wanted to be a counselor when I was younger, so it's been an interest of mine for a long time. A lot of people like to crank up the tunes and rock out to music when they train, but I listen to audiobooks, and almost always self-help. I had already listened to two of Terry Real's books, so when I was training for the Ironman, I started listening to *I Don't Want to Talk About It: Overcoming the Secret Legacy of Male Depression.* That book completely blew me away. It hit close to home as nothing else ever had.

Before the Ironman, I booked a counseling session with Terry. He was located in Boston, so it was easy to make arrangements. I went back for a second session with my wife and that's when it got heavy. We discussed areas of my past that I didn't want to talk about—things that I had swept under the rug a long time ago. By the end of those sessions, Terry recommended that I check myself into a Psychological Counseling Services (PCS) facility in Arizona, and my wife was threatening divorce if I didn't go. It was a punch to the gut that I wasn't prepared for.

I've always had anger issues. I would lose my temper. I'd often say things at work or get mad at my kids and then beat myself up over it the next day. I'd ruminate and wonder what the hell was wrong with me. My relationship with my wife wasn't always great, and there were times when I just didn't feel good. I would get down and I wouldn't know why, but I would just write it off as anxiety or me being intense and a go-getter. I wanted to be better and knew that I could be better—a better husband, father, and leader. But the reason they wanted me to go traced all the way back to my childhood.

My homelife growing up was not ideal. I knew that, but it was in the past. It had nothing to do with any of my current issues. At least that's what I thought, but nobody else saw it that way. The people in my life felt that I had to confront the past, and I didn't seem to have much choice, so two weeks after finishing the Ironman, I agreed to check myself into PCS. I had to go kicking and screaming, but I went.

The week was booked with about 65 hours of individual and group therapy sessions. It got intense. I did countless assessments, exercises, and assignments. One was called the trauma egg; a therapeutic exercise designed by Marilyn Murray, who was one of my therapists. It involved taking an inventory of all the traumatic moments in your life from birth right up until the present. I'd blow past everything that happened in my childhood and try to focus on more recent events, but just like during my sessions with Terry, they kept redirecting me back to my childhood.

One of the psychologists at PCS was a triathlete as well, and he knew that I had just finished the Ironman, so he took me under his wing. He probably spent more time with me than he should have during our one-on-ones. When he saw the results of my ACE (Adverse Childhood Experiences) test, he told me, "Given the abuse you went through as a child, you should be dead or in jail. You have a way of taking your issues and turning them into production."

I've watched people turn to drugs, alcohol, gambling, and sex when depressed. Others become violent, and some commit suicide, but I lost myself in workouts. A much healthier alternative that probably saved my life, but not one without its problems. For the first time, I saw how my training was getting in the way of other things in my life. How I would sneak in training and disguise it as something nice, so my family couldn't criticize me for not being around. I would pay for my wife to get an extra spa treatment so I could get a run in, or book a mountain bike ride for us to go on, just so I could stay longer and get my biking in for the day. I thought I was being slick and justified it by telling myself she could get an extra facial or massage, but I was really being selfish and manipulative. All she wanted was to spend more time with me.

The doctors at PCS felt that my childhood trauma was so severe that they diagnosed me with PTSD. I didn't believe it. My first reaction was denial. "I'm not worthy of that. That's a diagnosis for a warrior. I'm not a soldier. I didn't watch my brothers die out on the battlefield." What I didn't realize was that I was still doing what I had done my entire life: grouping myself in the category of being less-than, even with a freaking diagnosis!

I had been sweeping what happened to me during my child-hood under the rug. I chose not to acknowledge it. I ran away, literally. I dove into training and work, so I never improved or overcame these issues in my life that were the true source of my problems. They kept bubbling to the surface, and that had been holding me back for my entire life.

I've always known that we're all capable of more than we realize, but I was primarily talking about grit, determination, and perseverance related to what I could accomplish physically. Those more personal and relationship challenges were ones that I often didn't acknowledge and tried to ignore, but I was starting to learn that I couldn't run from them. They would all eventually surface. The storm that was my childhood had been

brewing for 48 years before I was forced to deal with it. I had
to approach it as I would so many of the other challenges I had
faced—the challenges that people said were impossible, and I
overcame.

How you react when in the storm is always a choice. For
my whole life, I was made to feel less than and told that I was
never enough, so I spent much of my childhood in survival
mode and playing the victim. Nothing changed for me until I
learned how to break out, take action, and make better choices
when facing adversity. Today I am living proof that it's not only
possible to survive the various storms, but to thrive by turning
those feelings of shame, anger, resentment, rejection, and fear
into happiness, joy, and an overall enthusiasm for life.

This book contains a lifetime of stories and lessons that
helped me to develop nine principles that have changed the way
that I face adversity today. This isn't a Band-Aid and there aren't
any quick-fix solutions in here. This process is meant to change
the way you think and approach everyday situations, because if
you wait until the storm hits to try and fix the issue, it's too late.
You need to do the work now to build a sturdy foundation and
develop the physical and mental resources required to handle
whatever life might throw at you.

It starts by dealing with your past, because you will never be
able to move forward if there are unresolved issues in your past
holding you back. Only then can you focus on the road ahead
and map out a plan for how to get there. Using my own life
as an example, the wins and the losses, I discuss how you can
find your purpose, set goals that you will follow through on,
break bad habits, and utilize your strengths to build up your
fortress, so you can win the day every day. I share the secrets
I've learned to help you create a positive mindset and develop
the confidence required to overcome any obstacle.

These storms in life are unavoidable. They come in all different forms, and often arrive unannounced, but one thing we know for sure is that they will arrive. I encountered a few while I was writing this very book. What set out to be a therapeutic book for me with a fairy-tale ending where I reconciled with my wife after a tragedy, saved my marriage, and lived happily ever after turned into something much different. Very little ever goes according to plan. The challenges I encountered during this process tested me in ways I couldn't have anticipated. In real time I was forced to put these strategies to the test and prove their effectiveness. The ending is one I could not have envisioned, but I couldn't be more satisfied with the way things turned out.

It doesn't matter what you do; you're never going to eliminate pressure, insecurity, doubt, fear, or anger, but you no longer need to let those feelings control you. Through preparation and changing the way you choose to show up every day, you can be better equipped to weather the next storm, whenever it may arrive.

CHAPTER 1
Make Peace with Your Past

"Every adversity, every failure, every heartbreak carries with it the seed of an equal or greater benefit."

—Napoleon Hill

For me, the storm had arrived early, and I'd been running from it since. For one of the exercises at PCS, I had to document the trauma that occurred before I was five years old. I did everything I could to get out of doing this. I got my master's in counseling and psych, and I've seen many counselors over the years, so I know which ones are good and which ones I can manipulate. That was easy, and it was almost a game to me at times, but those counselors at PCS were sharp. They were the best in the country and came recommended from someone else who was the best in the country, Terry Real. They wouldn't let me get out of it. Every time I tried to change the subject, I was redirected back to my childhood, but still, I couldn't remember a thing before the age of five, so I called up my mom to ask her.

It was a difficult call for me to make, and I think the conversation caught her off guard. Even though I had a great relationship with my mother and talked to her every day, we never discussed my childhood. On the phone, she told me that she couldn't remember anything, but a few hours later, she called me back, and I could tell she was crying on the other end of the line. She told me how when I was a baby, my father used to hold me under the faucet to get me to stop crying. I learned that my father basically waterboarded me when I was a baby. We can't do that to members of the Taliban today, but that's how my father got me to stop crying.

My mom was hysterical. "I feel so bad, Billy. I was such a bad mother to you. I should have done more." That was exactly what I was trying to avoid. I knew how bad she would feel and that she would blame herself if I brought this up.

"No, Mom. That's not why I called you. I know you did the best you could." She didn't have the resources or the tools at the time to protect me, but I think a part of her was in denial about the past as well. It wasn't good for her to dredge any of that up either and I hated to see her that upset.

After I hung up with my mother, I called up my sister, Kelly, to see what she might remember. Kelly was a year younger than me, and I love her to death today, but we were at each other's throats when we were kids. I had completely forgotten about it, but she told me how our dad had thrown me through a wall during an argument when I was a kid. I was probably eight or nine at the time. "I thought you were going to die," she told me. I know that my dad made me patch up the sheetrock after, but I still can't remember what the fight was over. It was another startling conversation, but not all that surprising either.

My dad was a Worcester firefighter, so he'd work for two days and then have two days off. Growing up, I knew his schedule better than him. I actually knew it months in advance. I'd study it and celebrate that time when he wasn't going to be home. I was in heaven when he wasn't there because I was free, but those days when he was home were a living hell, and I always had to watch my back.

He never broke any bones, and there was rarely any blood, but he'd grab me by the neck or slam my face into the ground. One time he stepped on my neck and held his foot there until I couldn't breathe. But more than the physical abuse, it was the bullying and the belittling that did the most damage.

Nothing was ever good enough for my father. He always gave me hell for my grades and wanted me to get all As and Bs, but he never went to one parent-teacher conference. And he never said a word when I busted my ass to get my grades up. That was crushing. Then there were the chores that I had to do around the house. Those never ended. I'd cut the grass, trim the hedges, and pull the weeds, all with hand tools. "Dad, why don't you buy an electric mower?"

"Why would I do that when I got you?"

That's how he looked at it. I was there to serve him. One day, he told me to go out and pick the poison ivy in the backyard. "Why don't we get some Roundup or weed killer?" I asked.

"No. You have to pull it out by the roots."

"I'm going to get poison ivy all over me."

"Then you better cover up."

Sure enough, I had poison ivy for two weeks. Every time I scratched myself it just made me hate him even more, but those were the kinds of things he did.

I got into my fair share of trouble as a kid, but sometimes I incurred his wrath without doing anything. He would come home some nights and rip me out of bed when I was sleeping, just because he had a bad day and needed to take it out on someone. It got to the point where I started planning ahead. I had a bunk bed in my room and got in the habit of sleeping on the top bunk and positioning the stuffed animals under the blanket on the bottom bunk, so it looked like that's where I was sleeping. I figured it would give me a little extra time to wake up and defend myself if he busted into the room. The only problem was that I was a lot higher up on the top bunk, so it was more painful when he ripped me out and threw me to the ground, but at the time, it seemed like the better option.

I tried to forget about those nights as I got older, but I clearly didn't because, as an adult, I would always have to sleep close to the door. I didn't even realize I was doing it at first, but that's what I did, whether I was in my bed, a hotel, or elsewhere. I don't know if I thought of it as a way to escape or what, but I finally connected the dots and realized it traced back to those nights when I would get ripped out of bed by my father.

Day or night, my father and I would always seem to go at it, and whenever he was mad at me for something, he wouldn't let it go. "Say you're sorry and tell me you won't do it again."

If I didn't say it, he would start poking me in the chest with his finger. He'd poke me again, again, and again. Finally, I got tired of it, so I'd talk back. "I'll say I'm sorry, but it's a lie because I'm really not sorry." That would usually result in me being brought to the floor, and he wouldn't let me up until I submitted.

"I'm the boss." That was something he said all the time. He'd walk around telling people that he was the boss. People would joke about it, and somebody even gave him a coffee mug with "I'm the boss" written on it, but it would drive me out of my mind. I would never tell him that he was the boss. Those words would never come out of my mouth.

"This is my house, and these are my rules, so if you don't like it, you can leave," and "Children should be seen and not heard." Those were two of his favorites, but the one thing he said to me that I'll never forget was how he never wanted us kids to have a better life than him because that wouldn't be fair. What father says that to their children? Even when I was young, I knew that I would make sure that my kids always had it better than me.

Not only was he selfish, but he was also a control freak, and he bossed me around just because he could. Whenever the streetlights came on at night and I wasn't home, I knew that I would be punished. If we were playing football in the park and I saw the lights go on, all my friends would joke, "We're not going to see Murph for another week."

And I always went home alone, not that my friends ever wanted to go with me. My father wasn't approachable. He would never talk to my friends or ask how they were. When I went over to my friend's houses, their parents would ask me questions and genuinely take an interest in me. My dad didn't care, and didn't allow me to have friends over anyway, which was fine by me because when he was there, the energy was toxic and the mood dark. I didn't want to be there either, so I had no problem hanging out at my friends' houses. If I was home, I knew that there would be more chores, more things to get in trouble for, and more times I would get yelled at. That's why I got perfect attendance in elementary school. Not because I was a being nerdy or even interested in school, I just didn't want to stay at home. So, it didn't matter if I had a cold, a fever, or felt like absolute death, I would always go to school.

Often what saved me more than being out of the house was my mother. I can say without a doubt that I would have gotten into way more conflicts with my father if my mother didn't step in when she found out I did something that would set him off. She always had my back and protected my sisters and me because she knew what would happen if my father got wind of what was going on. She would also take us out to McDonald's and Burger King, because my father wouldn't let us have any junk food. When he wasn't home, she sometimes let us splurge on ice cream. It was her way of trying to make things seem better and make up for the terrible home life we all had.

When I was 14, I tried to back up the car in our driveway, and I smashed up my dad's boat trailer. My mom told my father that she did it, and he yelled at her for a day straight, but she took the bullet for me.

I don't know if my parents were ever happy together—I certainly never saw it. It's hard for me to even picture it, given how mad he would get at her. My father never physically abused my mother. He would just degrade and belittle her almost daily. I used to tell myself that it was just the way things were back then, but that's not true. I had a lot of friends whose families came from a similar background, and it wasn't like that at home for them. I watched my friend's dads treat their wives with respect, but my father never did. There was no respect in my house.

My mother was a people pleaser and did her absolute best to try and keep the peace, but that was an impossible task. When my dad would talk down to her or degrade her, she never talked back. It was always a one-sided attack. She was clearly unhappy, but more than anything else, I think she was just numb to the verbal abuse.

Growing up, Kelly and I would watch some of the other kids come into school crying and depressed because their parents were getting divorced. Divorce wasn't that common back then, but it did happen. While other kids were pouring their hearts out to the guidance counselor, Kelly and I were asking ourselves, "Why the hell don't our parents just get divorced?" We even brought it up to our mom, but she didn't consider it an option. "Where would I go?" she would always say. "What am I going to do? I don't have a job. I don't have a car. I don't have any money." That was the old Irish-Catholic mentality. She had been married since she was 20. That was the life she had, and it was the life she had to live. That's how she thought, at least while I was in the house. They did eventually get divorced when I was 33. She finally reached her breaking point, and infidelity was the last straw, but that's how long it took.

Kelly and I may have been rooting for our parents to get divorced, but there was very little else we agreed on. I was a bully toward my sister, and in turn, she would get me in a lot of trouble, but she was the better person. She was way more mature than me. I was a jerk and despite how much I messed with her, she would never take it personally or throw anything in my face. But still, sometimes we would go at it. After one fight with my sister, our dad pulled me out of bed, held me down, and tried to get my sister to punch me in the face. Whether he realized it or not, he pitted us against each other. She was as shocked as I was. She didn't want to do it, but he made her. "Just hit him!" So, she did. Pretty soon, she was in tears, pleading with my dad to let her stop. The whole thing just got me so pissed off, but it was weird because I felt bad for her at the same time. As he told her to hit me harder, I could tell that she was holding back. Eventually, she just ran out of the room. My dad let up and proceeded to ridicule and berate me. That was a humiliating moment for me, and it's still embarrassing for me to talk about, which is why hardly anybody knows about it. I was held down while my sister tooled me in the face.

I saw all of the love in my friends' homes and got used to just not having that at my house, but I always hoped that things would change. I'd keep going back to the well and try to win over my dad, and every once in a while, I'd see a glimmer of hope.

When I was 10, he asked me if I wanted to go with him to sign up for Little League. I was in shock. "Really? You never let me sign up." That caught me completely off guard. He never wanted to pay the $40, so I'd have to ask my mother or grandfather to take me to sign up, but he suddenly seemed to have a change of heart. I was so excited on the drive over. We got there, went through the process, and on the way home, just for a brief while, I thought things might be different. "Thanks for signing me up," I told him.

"Oh, you'll be working that off." We weren't even in the car for more than five minutes when he told me that.

You son of a bitch! I didn't say a word for the rest of the ride home. I had no idea what he would ask me to do later, but I'm sure he had something in mind, because he always had an agenda. I was his bitch. That's what he saw me as. I hated him so much, but that's how it went with him.

That glimmer of hope would be short lived and gone in the blink of an eye, so it was almost like nothing had ever happened. Every good deed or olive branch came with a catch. He used to take me fishing and hunting sometimes, and then we'd get home, and he'd make me do more chores. "I took you fishing; you owe me." Eventually, I stopped going with him, and then he would try to guilt-trip me. "I was going to take you fishing. Why didn't you want to go?"

It was a no-brainer for me. "I don't want to because you're going to make me do a whole bunch of chores when we get back."

Everything was conditional, and if he felt like you owed him, then you owed him. I don't even know if he liked me tagging along with him on those trips. It certainly wasn't father-son bonding. I'm not sure why he bothered to bring me. Maybe he just wanted the company. He wasn't a guy with a lot of friends, and it wasn't a mystery to me why.

Things started to change for me at home when I got a little older and stronger. Eventually, I started lifting, and I got bigger. When I was 13, I told him, "If you keep doing this, one day I'm going to beat the hell out of you." He almost broke my neck for that one.

I found myself getting bolder. There were a couple of times when I went into the bedroom and confronted him for the way he was talking to my mother, but when I was 16, it finally happened. I remember because the Red Sox were playing the A's in the playoffs, and Roger Clemens was pitching. I went into my youngest sister Kristina's room to watch the game. She was only five at the time. She didn't want me in there and ran to tell my dad. "Billy, get the hell out of her room!" he said.

"You're not even watching the Sox? What kind of man are you?"

That got him upset. He came after me for questioning his manhood. But I was ready, and this time I decked him. Once I got him on the ground, I put him in a headlock and said, "If you struggle or fight me, I'm going to punch you in the face." He kept resisting for a while, but I squeezed harder until he tapped out, so I let him go.

I left the house that day, and I never stayed there permanently again. I wasn't going to do his chores anymore or listen to him blame me for everything, so I bounced around and stayed with my aunt or friends or girlfriends until I finished high school. After leaving home, I moved on from childhood, but I never confronted those demons, and as I got older, I pretended they didn't exist.

It took the therapists at PCS for me to make that connection and discover the true source of so many of my issues. Whenever I wanted to focus on what I thought was the trauma at the source of my troubles, they redirected me back to my childhood. That happened over and over again. When I watched the doctors and clinicians break down into tears after hearing stories about the abuse a poor kid had to endure, I realized that kid they were talking about was me. I never saw it that way, and never felt bad for myself, but if I heard those same stories about someone else's kid, I would be horrified. That's what made me realize how close-minded I had been, and that I had to care for my inner child the same way I would someone else's innocent child. I had to learn how to have the same empathy for myself that I would for others.

Even if you had a great childhood, there may be something else in your past that's the source of current issues and holding you back from reaching your true potential. But you can't fix the problem if you don't know the source. If the lights go out in your house, you can tell yourself the light bulb needs replacing all you want, but that does you no good if you really blew a fuse. Here is a simple way to begin this process:

EXERCISE

Make a list of all the baggage from your past that you cling to. Give yourself plenty of time. Set aside 20 or even 30 minutes if necessary, so you can stir up some of those things you've tried to forget. What storm have you gone through that's still creating obstacles in your life and preventing you from living the life you want? What are you sweeping under the rug? What lies are you telling yourself about the way things are? What skeletons are in your closet that you chose to ignore? Being open-minded, looking at things from another point of view, and having empathy for yourself and what you've been through can help you finally see what might be hiding under the surface. The point of writing it all down is not so you can dwell on it, but so you can release it! But you can't release what you aren't aware of or refuse to acknowledge, so self-awareness is the first step.

Look for the Silver Linings

I recently talked with my therapist about my childhood. After thinking about the beatings, the belittling, the shaming and constantly being made to feel less than, I was really starting to develop ill will toward him. I didn't want to go down that road because I knew how it can bring you down, suck your energy, and ruin your day if you let it. I never used to talk about any of this stuff, but since PCS, I've discussed it with a few of my coaches and therapists. However, my therapist told me something that I hadn't even thought of before. "You know," she said. "Your father gave you one of the greatest gifts you've ever received."

It took me a while to wrap my head around that. I was depressed as a kid, and I don't think it's a mystery where my anger issues come from, but then it hit me. *Damn, she's right!* Being forced to live in survival mode taught me how to get ahead. The reason that I am the way I am and the reason why I experienced success in certain areas of my life can be traced directly back to what I went through as a kid. I wouldn't want to go through it again, and I wouldn't want to see anybody else go through that, because there are so many different ways it could have led to disaster, but I wouldn't be where I am today had I not.

I hated being home so much, I got out of the house every chance I got. At nine, I would follow the paperboy around after he came to my house. I'd throw some papers in people's yards. Finally, he asked, "You wanna help me? I'll pay you." By the following year, I had three paper routes and was getting up at 4:30 a.m. seven days a week to deliver papers. During the week, I'd finish up at 6:00 a.m. and go back to sleep for an hour before going to school. We had a lot of snowstorms and blizzards in Worcester back then, but I never missed a day. That's not completely true, because there was one day where the papers never arrived because of the snow, but if there were papers to deliver, I delivered them. I was friends with most all of the other paperboys, and nobody else wanted to deliver papers in the snow (sometimes their parents just didn't let them), but I took that responsibility seriously. I don't know if it was pride or what, but I didn't want to let down my customers. I couldn't ride my bike on the mornings when there were more than six inches of snow, so I had to walk, and that added another hour and a half to the route. That meant I had to get up earlier, but school was often delayed or canceled, so I didn't have anywhere else to be.

I was the only paperboy out there recruiting new customers. I would knock on doors and try to get people to subscribe to *The Telegram Gazette*. I figured they were on my route anyway, and if I had more customers then I would make more money. I was a 12-year-old entrepreneur who was learning the power of money. I was making $400 a week in cash; much more than any of my friends. I had the best bike in the neighborhood—the one with the white mag wheels back when mag wheels had to be specially ordered. By the time I was 14, I had purchased a motorboat. Yes, a boat. We lived off Lake Quinsigamond, and I had a friend who had a dock, so that's where I kept it. We used it for water skiing, and as a way to pick up girls. I kept that boat all the way through college. *The Telegram Gazette* even did an article on me for being the model paperboy who was able to acquire all of these things with money I made from my paper route.

It wasn't just delivering papers. I was an altar boy, too. Our family didn't go to church, but I'd go with my friends, and some of them were altar boys, so I was like, "Sign me up." Other times, I'd go knock on the neighbor's door to see if I could cut their grass or shovel their driveway. I didn't care if I got paid. I'd even lie to my dad and tell him that I had an altar boy meeting or practice just so I could get the hell out of the house.

As I got older, what I enjoyed more than anything else was sports. I played Little League, and I tried to sign up for football a year early. Baseball and football were my sports, but we also played street hockey, and then when the pond froze in the winter, we'd go out on the ice to play. I loved sports, but I was never as good an athlete as Kelly, who ended up being voted "best athlete" in her class. She played soccer, field hockey, and softball, and was good at all of them. My friends always gave me a hard time that my sister was the better athlete. I would never admit it at the time, but I rooted for her.

What's funny was that a few years after I left home, I got a call from my youngest sister Kristina when she was around 10 because our dad didn't want to get her a glove or sign her up for softball. I didn't want her to have to go through what I did, so I took her to the sporting goods store to get a glove. She wanted to become a pitcher, so I used to practice with her after school. I had forgotten all about that story for a long time until she reminded me. It may sound counterintuitive, but I became more generous because of what I experienced at home. Our father had mellowed out after I left the house, so Kristina didn't have it nearly as bad as Kelly and I, but I knew that it wasn't easy for her either, so I did my best to be there for her in ways that our father would not be. Something else that came out of my childhood was optimism. No matter how bad things got, I remained optimistic. I always felt that things would work out in the end. I didn't realize it at the time, but that might have had something to do with my wanting to be the complete opposite of my father. He was so pessimistic and negative that I wanted to be positive just so I wouldn't be like him.

Good or bad, and wherever they came from, those traits are what helped me survive because I was always last in the pecking order. I knew that I wasn't the best, and that feeling was reinforced at home, so whether it was school or sports, I felt that I always had to work harder than everyone else. I would stay after class to get help from teachers. And that was just so I could get my grades up to average and keep up with the quote-unquote smart kids. As early as middle school, I sought out coaches to see what they could teach me so I could get that edge or find that angle. I devoured every single sports magazine and article I could get my hands on.

That drive to prove that I wasn't less than created a competitive fire that made me want to be the best at everything I did. That helped me develop determination, grit, and competitiveness at a very early age. I forced myself to go to school every day just so I didn't have to stay at home, and that became a habit that stuck with me for the rest of my life. I never missed a day of work. When it came to sports, I played hurt, or until I just couldn't go anymore. That wasn't always a good idea, but it's just how I was wired. But when I would encounter storms later in life, and suffer from anxiety and depression, I wouldn't self-destruct. Instead, I threw myself into the same habits that got me through my childhood—competition, athletics, work, and self-improvement.

Of course, my therapist was only speculating when she said my father's treatment was a gift. Neither of us will ever know for sure how things would have turned out if I was raised differently. I've got to believe that DNA has something to do with the people we become, but there is no doubt in my mind that my environment hardened me. I've come to learn that there is a silver lining to almost every situation. Look hard enough, change your perception, or just view things with an open mind, and you will find those silver linings.

A big part of making peace with your past is learning how to forgive yourself. Living with regret is one of the hardest things you will have to do, so you need to release that. That's where so many people struggle, but one way to do that is to focus on those silver linings, because there is always a bright spot, whether you choose to see it or not. Instead of dwelling on the negative and what went wrong, ask yourself, "What did I learn?" "What was the lesson?" "How can I benefit from this?"

EXERCISE

Go back to that list you created of all your baggage during the last exercise and try looking at it from a different perspective. Instead of focusing on the negative, look for the silver linings. In what ways have your past mistakes shaped who you've become in a positive way? What's so powerful about this exercise is that it doesn't always have to be about the past. You can do this the next time something goes wrong or doesn't go your way. Instead of getting down or playing the victim, try looking at it from a different perspective. You want to take time to digest the feelings and wrap your head around what's actually happening, but when the dust settles, ask yourself: *What good can come out of this situation and how can I benefit?*

If there is a first step to this process of self-development, it's looking inward and laying all the cards out on the table, so you can be honest with yourself. Acknowledging your baggage, learning to forgive yourself, and finding the silver linings will help you heal and move forward instead of being stuck living in the past. We've all endured a series of storms, some big and others small, but they all make an impact and leave an impression. Pretending they didn't happen or trying to forget won't undo any of the damage done. The past can be painful, but it's something we all must confront if we want to improve. We all have regrets, and the faster we can make peace, the sooner we can clear our minds and move on.

CHAPTER 2
What Is Your Purpose?

"He who has a why to live for can bear almost any how."
—Friedrich Nietzsche

My upbringing was also what first got me interested in psychology, even if I didn't have a clue what that was at first. All I wanted to do was figure out why my father was so messed up. For as long as I can remember, I always took an interest in the mental side of things. Whether it's life or sports, it always comes down to the mental side and your attitude. Talk to any winning coach in any sport, and they'll tell you that it's about getting knocked down and being able to get back up. What was it about some people that motivated them to get up when adversity struck them?

I'm probably the only kid on record who used the money he made delivering papers to buy subliminal cassette tapes. I saw them advertised on an infomercial, so I ordered them. It was just one more thing that could possibly give me an edge or a leg up. These were tapes you would listen to at night, and they were all about self-confidence and self-esteem. It might have been the placebo effect, but I like to think they worked at the time. Either way, that was my introduction to the world of personal development.

I may have never missed a day of school, but I had zero interest in what I was learning until I took my first psychology class in high school, and that's when I knew what I wanted to do with my life. People loved to take psychology, so that class filled up fast. And we were bummed that we had to wait until we were sophomores to sign up, but I made sure that class was first on my list. I loved learning about how we think and what makes people tick. The concepts were fascinating to me. When I went to college at Worcester State, I changed my major four times, but I always gravitated back toward psychology. Once I got past all of the entry-level courses in other subjects, I could really focus on it.

When I was a junior, I took a job in the Worcester Department of Youth Services working in the juvenile lockup division, where I counseled the inmates and the kids who were recently released. I loved the people I worked with. It was a brotherhood, and I'm still in touch with some of the colleagues and clinicians. Together, we worked our asses off to come up with treatment plans to help those kids rebuild their lives, but often we were fighting an uphill battle.

A lot of these kids were hardcore gangbangers who had been locked up for some gross, disgusting, and horrific things, including murder and rape. However, you wouldn't always know it just by talking to them. That's what really helped me to understand just how much we are shaped by our environment. I bet if those same kids were brought up in a healthy environment and raised in a loving home, they would be some of the best athletes and smartest kids at their school.

You had to be careful about getting too close to them. Boundaries had to be set because you didn't want any of them looking you up or coming around your neighborhood or your family. But it was a big deal when you saw a kid who had a chance of getting out, and I always found myself rooting for my favorites. Whenever one of them experienced a breakthrough or made a significant improvement to get out of the system and better their lives, it was one of the most rewarding experiences of my life, but the reality was that so few of them changed. A few managed to get to college or land a legitimate job, but that was pretty rare. Most went right back where they came from and did the same things that had gotten them in trouble the first time. Many of them even got killed, but it wasn't always their fault. The state would put them right back in the same environment, so what choice did they have? These kids were stuck in a vicious cycle, and I felt powerless to do anything as I watched the same tragic story unfold again and again. That was frustrating and, over time, it wore me down. After five years, I realized that I couldn't make a career out of this. I started thinking about going in another direction, but I was in my mid-20s and still had no idea what I wanted to do with my life.

It the summer of 1997, I had just earned my master's degree and considered getting my doctorate in psychology, but I didn't think I was capable. I didn't think I could write well enough or that I was smart enough to put together a solid thesis. I didn't even talk to anyone about it because I would have been

embarrassed to hear some people say that it was not a legitimate option for me, so I quickly talked myself out of it. I had
lost my direction. I didn't have a purpose, and as a result, I was
drifting into a dangerous territory.

My roommate and I used to take bets on sports games out of our
apartment. I learned very quickly that the public never wins—at
least 60 percent of the time they don't, which was enough to make
us some decent money. I had figured out a way to bet against the
lines, but once we started to make a little bit of money, it became
a headache, because when people lose, you have to track them
down, and they don't want to pay. That can turn ugly extremely
fast, especially when dealing with friends who owe you money. I
was in over my head, and I didn't like what I had to do to make
that business work. Confront, confront, confront—that's what
the job was all about when people wouldn't pay.

Meanwhile, my routine consisted of going to work, going
to the gym, and then going out to party—sometimes all on the
same day. I did all the stupid things that kids in their early 20s
do, but a part of me still had the attitude that I had to keep
working, even though I had no idea what I was working toward.
There were times when I was out all night, and then would hit
the gym hungover, or worse, drunk. It stopped being fun, and
I was starting to get myself into trouble.

I grew up around street fights. I always got into my share of
fights on the playground because that's how we handled things.
As I got older, that carried over to barroom brawls. My friends
and I were frequently getting into melees, and I was the angriest
of the bunch, so I seemed to get into the lion's share. I wouldn't
back down. I thought I was the guy who would swoop in and
take everyone out, but in reality, I was definitely not that guy, so
I got my ass kicked a lot. With maturity and a little more wisdom, I eventually learned to avoid getting myself into situations

that could escalate, but that didn't happen for a while. I was on a path to disaster, and finally one Sunday afternoon, it struck.

I had been drinking down at the lake with my friends. When we left around 4:00 p.m. I made the mistake of thinking I was okay to drive because I didn't have that far to go. I dropped off my friend and started to make the mile drive back to my house. I can't remember exactly what happened but learned after the fact that while driving down the main drag in a residential part of town, I veered off the side of the road, clipped a few parked cars, flipped over my truck, smacked into a telephone pole, somehow flew out of the car, and landed on the pavement 20 feet away from the truck.

I should have been dead, but I came to in the middle of the street. When I got to my feet and realized that I could move, I saw that I had a few cuts, and there was a lot of blood, but I wasn't hurt. I was in shock. Nothing felt real. My mind raced trying to piece together what had just happened. When I saw my truck all smashed up and lying on its side, I realized how everything could have easily been so much worse. I should never have gotten behind the wheel. It was broad daylight, but it wasn't a crowded area of town, so luckily I didn't hurt anybody.

A firetruck was the first to arrive on the scene. I happened to know Kevin, one of the firemen. My dad was his boss. I knew a lot of the guys in the department—many of them were involved in Pop Warner football when I was a kid. Even if they thought my dad was an asshole, they liked me, and we had a good relationship, so they looked out for me. That's what Kevin did that day, and I'm grateful, even though I didn't deserve any special treatment after what had just happened. As the paramedics examined me, Kevin somehow managed to keep the cops at bay, so they couldn't question me or give me a blood test before I was taken to the hospital. Once there, I remembered the layout from my paper route days, so I snuck down the back stairs, and left.

When you're young, you think you're invincible, even when you're old enough to know better, but immaturity can cause us to act like idiots who think we're above the law. I put a lot of people in harm's way that day. I was lucky that nobody got hurt. That hammered the point home for me not to get behind the wheel if I had been drinking and to always call for help if I needed it. That's something I'm a huge stickler for today with my kids. I tell them that no matter what they do, they won't get in trouble if they call me for help or to come pick them up. I get so nervous because I know how dangerous it is, and how easily things can go wrong—I witnessed it firsthand. That, for me, was a wake-up call. I was starting to feel like a failure, and something needed to change. I didn't want to squander what was clearly an undeserved second chance. There was one problem: I didn't know my purpose.

Before you do anything else, you need to find your purpose. That doesn't mean you have to sit around and wait for some big, life-changing event to point you in the right direction. If you don't know your why, finding it is often as simple as examining the voids in your life and looking at how you want to be more fulfilled. Other times, the answer is right in front of you. I certainly didn't realize it at the time, but there were signs pointing me in the right direction every step of the way. Those signs are all around; you just have to know where to look.

If you're struggling to find your why, and you don't know where to start, try following these steps that I learned the hard way.

Let Your Values Be Your Guide
I had to turn over a new leaf. It started by getting out of the bookie business. That's not who I was and it's not what I wanted

to do. I also knew that I didn't want to stay in Worcester. Part of me always wanted to be on the west coast, so I made the decision to move out to California. I had no idea what I was looking for, but it was time for me to get the hell out of dodge and do some soul searching. I officially left the Department of Youth Services and cashed out my state pension early. That came with huge penalties, so I only got $3,000 instead of $5,000, but when you're 26, you don't care about those things.

My grandmother lived out in San Clemente, so that's where I went to right the ship. I purchased a car and had it shipped out while I flew across the country. I lived with her for the first couple of weeks and then got my own place, but first I needed to find a job.

Since I was a kid, I had always thought about becoming a cop, so I set out to join the California Highway Patrol, and I did well on both the physical and written tests. The only issue was that I had to wait six months to establish residency before I could enroll in the academy. The idea of being a cop grounded me, and immediately I felt a difference, but I also needed to make a living, so my uncle got me a job in the mortgage industry as a telemarketer. He was in the mortgage business and ran his own brokerage with my aunt, but it was a small two-person shop, so he couldn't give me a job. Instead, he set me up with some colleagues who he came up in the business with.

I had no idea what I was doing. I didn't even know there was a "t" in mortgage when I started. I was at the very bottom of the barrel. What they had me doing was worse than cold calls. They gave me a box of loan applications, 1003s, and set me up in a spare room with a phone, headset, and computer and told me to generate business.

What you don't know won't hurt you, and what I didn't know then was that most of these 1003s were over three years old. I was phoning people who had applied for a mortgage three years earlier. I would've been better off flipping through the phone book and randomly picking out names. If someone asked me to do that today, I'd say, "You're crazy," but back then, it must have been my enthusiasm, passion, or something that came through on the phone because I was able to get customers. I liked what I was doing. I did it well and started making good money, so I decided not to follow through with the California Highway Patrol.

I was loving life for a while. Living in Orange County was an amazing experience. I was in a much better place than I had been when back home in Massachusetts and, even though I had stumbled upon it by accident, I finally had direction and a career path. I also met some great people and grew very close to the core crew I hung out with. One was my boss, but most were people who I saw every day at the gym and would work out with. They were from all over the country—Ohio, Maryland, and even Massachusetts, which was where my boss was from.

However, something about California felt different than back home. Whenever I drifted outside my circle or hung out with some of the locals, it didn't feel like they were my people. They didn't seem like they truly care about each other. They had this surfing, fly-by-the-seat-of-your-pants mentality where whoever was around was around and whoever wasn't was out of sight and out of mind. Nobody cared about loyalty, at least not the way that I thought about loyalty, particularly when it came to relationships. Most every girl I dated didn't think twice about hanging out with an ex or hooking up with someone else. I don't know if it was a trendy Orange County thing, but that really bothered me.

I knew deep down inside that California wasn't the kind of place where I would ever want to raise a family, and I knew that one day I wanted to be a father and have a family. I'd go over to my friends' houses growing up, and they were close to their families, so I became close to their families. There was a close-knit family dynamic back east that was missing where I lived in California. I also started to miss the little things: Dunkin Donuts, my Boston sports teams, playing Park League football, and hanging out with the boys. But more than anything else, it was my family that I wanted to get back to. Obviously, I didn't want to relive my childhood or the abuse, but I was close to my mother, sisters, aunts, uncles, and friends. So, in July 1999, after two years, I packed up my stuff, said my goodbyes, and drove cross-country back to Massachusetts. I had told myself, and everyone else, that it was only temporary and that I would head back to California eventually, but I had no idea what I was going to do.

For as aimless as I felt, my values were keeping me in check, no matter how many times I veered off course. I may have been a slow learner, and it took me a while before I stepped up on my own, but I stopped doing things that were not in line with my values time and time again. It would have been easier to make money in the gambling world. It would have been easier to stay out in California and not worry about responsibility or commitment, but I didn't take the easy path, and it led me somewhere even better.

We all have that voice in our head telling us what is right and wrong—what is in line with our core values, and what goes against what we believe in. We're pressured to cross that line all the time, be it to make more money, or get into the good graces of people we want to impress. Sometimes it can be difficult to listen to that voice and do the right thing because it's often the harder thing to do, but the more you listen to that voice, the more it will steer you where you need to go and help you find your way, and eventually, your why.

EXERCISE

What are your core values? If you don't know, take the time to come up with three. Throughout the years, my why has changed, but it always remains tethered to one of my three core values. And if it's not, that's a good indication that you need to re-evaluate either your why or your values.

Pursue Your Passion

When I arrived back home in Massachusetts, I tried picking up where I left off in the mortgage industry because I really liked what I was doing. The money was good, so it was the best option available. I had worked with some great people who showed me the ropes, and I saw that I had the potential to make some decent money. It wasn't long before I landed a job in the subprime world at Ameriquest. I thought the gambling industry was shady, but this was worse. It was straight out of *The Big Short*.

This was in 2000, when the subprime market was at its peak, leading up to the housing crisis a few years later, but anybody working in that world could already see that there was trouble on the horizon. People were getting loans who had no assets, no income, and horrible credit. These loans were awful because of the way they were structured. The lenders were banking on clients continually refinancing and living off that money they pulled out. Picture your $200,000 mortgage going from 8 percent to 13 percent overnight. They were just setting people up to be foreclosed on, and these were single mothers and working-class people. Yeah, they signed the paperwork, but they didn't know what they were signing. They put their faith and trust in people who were supposed to be advisors.

I didn't have a clue what I was walking into, but once I started working there, I saw how completely unethical the whole thing was. There were a lot of shenanigans, and I knew right away that I did not want to be a part of that world. It didn't feel right, and I didn't feel good about myself. I wanted to be an A-paper lender, which meant working with the people who could qualify, or who I could help qualify, not the people who were handed a loan because they had a pulse. No matter how much money I saw some of these guys make writing these loans that were just awful, I knew it was ethically wrong, and there was no satisfaction in any of it. It wasn't aligned with my values, and it certainly wasn't my passion, so after six months I left. I didn't want to completely leave the mortgage industry. There was something about it that I still liked, so that's what I set out to reconnect with.

I always enjoyed reading about athletes, particularly those who made it through the school of hard knocks and managed to emerge intact on the other side. I identified with those athletes who could endure difficult times and then perform on the highest level. That evolved into me gravitating toward other people's success stories in all walks of life. I never got jealous or was envious of another's accomplishments. If anything, I was in awe and wanted to learn from those people. That's kind of surprising considering that I was taught "money was the root of all evil." If anything, I grew up to believe the complete opposite. I was fascinated by how people were able to achieve at such a high level and wanted to learn how they got ahead.

So, when I first got into the mortgage business and spent all day talking to people on the phone as a telemarketer, what interested me more than anything else were their stories. It probably had something to do with my background in counseling and psych, or maybe it was just the nature of the job, but people would open up and start telling me all about themselves. I created files on all of these potential clients to give to the loan officers, but none of them paid any attention, and they rarely called any of those people back. That got me so frustrated that I decided to do the only thing I could to make myself feel better—I become a loan officer.

Back then, you didn't have to be certified or anything, so I was able to make an easy transition. And I still loved listening to people's stories. I never wanted to be an order taker or someone who just rattled off my rate and tried to negotiate numbers. I never bought into any of that. I wanted to know what drove people and learn what they were trying to do with their lives. Once I learned what was going on in other people's lives, I realized that my job went beyond just the numbers. It felt like I was playing a small role in helping other people live out their own success stories. I was helping people finance their American Dream. I was given the responsibility of helping them acquire what was their biggest asset, their house, and also their biggest liability, their mortgage. I understood the magnitude of the potential impact I could make for people and families. That gave me a feeling like very little else in this world could, and that's what I was missing when working in the subprime world, so after leaving that horrific job, I was able to get back on track and find a job that allowed me to pursue that passion and recapture that feeling all over again. I've been in the business for over 20 years now, and that's something that I never lost sight of.

When you're a kid, nobody dreams about growing up to be in the mortgage business. It's not a sexy profession. I can round up the top 200 mortgage brokers in the country, and not one of them will tell you that they planned their career trajectory from the beginning. They all started out doing something else.

It was the same with me. I'm not exaggerating when I say that what I do for a living today is my passion. I loved my job at the Department of Youth Services and really set out to make a difference for some of those kids, but that was an uphill battle with a very low success rate. And frankly, it was painful to see so many kids never make it out. Maybe I would have been successful in another form of sales, but I doubt I would have been able to make the same impact, and I certainly wouldn't have the same passion doing what I do now. I still feel the same exhilaration today that I did over 20 years earlier when I was making cold calls. It's what keeps me going, and the fact that I've been able to make a career out of my passion is the reason why I have been successful.

A lot of people ignore or neglect their passion in favor of what they think they should be doing with their lives, only to realize that what they should be doing doesn't make them happy. That only makes it more difficult to find their purpose. When you're struggling to find your why, try this exercise to reconnect with your passion.

EXERCISE

What keeps you going? If money wasn't an issue, how would you choose to spend your time? What do you love to do? Make a list of all the things that bring you joy and fulfilment. Now, see if you can find something that lives at the crossroad where your passion and your values meet. It doesn't have to be a career, but you want to find ways to bring some kind of enjoyment to your days. If you don't yet know your why, listen to that voice in your head, stay true to your values, follow your passion, and sooner or later, it will reveal itself.

Finding Your Why

Shortly after I returned from California, I learned that an old girlfriend who I been seeing off and on was pregnant. My world was completely rocked, but in a good way. I had always wanted to be a father, and even though this was not something we planned for, I knew that I needed to do everything right from that moment forward. I needed to be the best version of myself for my child. My life was never going to be the same, and I suddenly realized what that void was that I had been feeling.

Up until that point, I had been driven primarily by competitiveness. When I was a kid, I worked my ass off to prove that I wasn't a victim of my circumstances and that I wasn't less than. In retrospect, I succeeded, but at the time, I was always looking for more, and that's what drove me. Once I was out of the house and I had graduated from college, I still wanted to be better, but I felt that I had much less to prove. As a result, I had no direction. I had no why. That's the reason I went off course.

When I learned that I was going to be a father, that was the first time that I ever put together a life plan and actively thought about my purpose. It was instantaneous—like a light switch went off, and suddenly I could see exactly what I needed to do so clearly. I knew that there was no way that my child was going to grow up the same way as me, and I did everything in my power to make sure I would be able to provide that kid with the best life possible. My son Kameron was born in April 2000, and I am still driven to be the best dad that I can possibly be.

It took me a long time to figure out my purpose or my why. It takes some people even longer, and some people go through their entire lives without ever learning their why. Over time, people grow complacent, get used to their surroundings or become content. Or sometimes, like in my case, people experience a life-changing event that gives them direction. And that event doesn't have to be positive. It could be a health scare. How many times has someone turned their life around and committed themselves to live differently after suffering a heart attack or winning a battle against cancer? That why is important because if you want to change your life, you have to want to change. It's not going to happen on its own, so you will need a reason why, and it's got to be a good one or else you won't have a reason to follow through.

Think of it this way: you would probably never consider running into a burning building, but if your child was stuck in the second-floor bedroom, you wouldn't think twice about doing whatever you needed to do to rescue that child. When you're motivated and want something badly enough, you can accomplish almost anything.

Your why is unique to you. It's not what someone else wants you to do or thinks you should do. You hear stories all the time about people who pursued a certain job or degree because their parents expected it of them, or they thought that it would be an easy path to success, only to realize at 40 that they hate what they do. That's often a result of them following someone else's why. Granted, this can be difficult to navigate if you come from a family of doctors and you have no desire to go to medical school, but if you want to achieve true success and happiness, your why has to be yours and not anyone else's.

Your why lives at the intersection of your values and your passion. It becomes the reason you get up in the morning and work so hard. It's your drive and your motivation. It's your fuel that will keep you going and allow you to follow through to achieve your goals. If you're going to have success, and be able to thrive in the storm, you will absolutely need to identify your why. That's non-negotiable.

It's Never Too Late to Find Your Purpose

Back in 2005, Louise Thaxton thought of herself as an average loan officer working out of her small hometown in Louisiana. This was a few years before I ever met her and started working with her. And we probably never would have worked together had it not been for a disaster. She was in her 50s at the time, but she didn't love the job, so she was looking to get out of the mortgage business and find her passion. Her faith was always important to her, so she wanted to find something more spiritually rewarding. She wasn't sure what that was, but before she had a chance to figure it out, disaster struck. Everything changed in September of that year on one dark and stormy night, as she likes to refer to it.

Hurricane Rita devasted the state of Louisiana, and with it the family farm that provided Louise and her husband three-quarters of their income. They had no insurance, so their lives changed almost overnight. Anyone who owns and runs their own farm knows that it's not a job, it's a lifestyle. Louise had never once considered that she could lose the farm, and was willing to do whatever it took to maintain that lifestyle. "Get up, gear up, show up, and do the work," was what she said. Louise wouldn't be able to leave her job just yet. If anything, she actually had to figure out how to make a little bit more money, while they rebuilt the farm.

Louise's father and stepfather were both veterans, so she had an appreciation and understanding for military culture. Fort Polk was a small army town just south of where she lived in Louisiana. Even though she joked that she couldn't spell "V.A." at the time, she made an attempt to tap into that market by providing veterans with V.A. loans, which are 100 percent financed loans with no mortgage insurance that are available only to veterans. She reached out to a local real estate agent whom she had done a small deal with earlier that year. That agent introduced her to a young man who had just returned from Iraq and was in the market for a home. As she sat across the table and listened to him talk about what he went through, her eyes welled with tears, and she realized that she owed it to him to do this right.

After closing that deal, Louise met with more and more veterans and logged a tremendous number of miles going back and forth to Fort Polk. She became fascinated by their stories and loved listening to them talk. Slowly, she began to learn about what they referred to as the military-civilian divide, which describes the disconnect veterans feel when returning to the general population. Less than 0.4 of 1 percent of Americans serve in the military, compared to almost 10 percent during WWII. Add to that how serving in the military has become a generational occupation, and very few civilians understand the nature of this divide. Even though many of them recognize the importance of supporting our returning veterans, they don't know how to help. Meanwhile, on average, 22 veterans take their own lives every day, which is a staggering number. She realized that the military community needed a watchdog to step in and help take care of those who had sacrificed to fight for our country. Louise took it upon herself to become an expert, not only on V.A. loans, but also military culture, so she could help bridge that growing divide.

One year after Hurricane Rita, there was a huge deployment of troops to Afghanistan. When that happens, spouses go home to be with their families—they don't buy houses. Since Fort Polk was a small army town, business dried up. Bossier City, Louisiana, was two hours north of where Louise lived, and that was an air force town where the majority of their residents didn't deploy. She saw an opportunity and started making the 110-mile commute each way three times a week to stir up new business. At that point, she was committed and willing to do whatever it took. In her mind, the sacrifice was nothing compared to that of the military community she served.

By the time the family farm was up and running again, Louise had quadrupled her business. She went from closing five to seven transactions a month in a town of 2,900 people to closing 25 to 30 in a military community of 8,000. She was no longer looking to get out of the mortgage industry, because she had finally found her calling. She achieved tremendous success, but it was never about the money. Rarely is money ever a strong enough why. You need something that connects to your heart, and that can bring everything together to serve as the flashpoint that allows your light to burn incredibly bright.

Louise started going above and beyond in her role as a loan officer by hosting events and reaching out to the community. It was through her network that she met Sean Parnell, a veteran and author who wrote the book *Outlaw Platoon* about his experience as an infantryman during the war in Afghanistan. It was a chance meeting that must have been fate because a few years later, they joined forces to create the American Warrior Initiative, a nonprofit designed to help bring awareness to our veterans and veteran-related causes. They work to give our active-duty military, disabled veterans, and first responders a helping hand by doing everything from taking care of home repairs to providing veterans with service dogs. The whole time, Louise has continued to increase her business, and she is now one of the top mortgage originators in the country.

Louise Thaxton was in her early 50s when she discovered her passion. Today, she's a mother of five with 17 grandchildren and four great-grandchildren and has no desire to slow down or retire. She is living proof that it's never too late to find your why. When you love what you do, you never work a day in your life, and Louise is determined to keep doing what she does until the day she dies.

* * *

We all feel lost at times. It's easy to let the storm set you adrift, and leave you feeling helpless, but it's important to remember that you are the one in control. Even if your destination is not visible, or you don't yet know where you need to go, your values, your passion, and your why will serve as your North Star to lead you out of the chaos and into calmer waters. It doesn't matter how old you are, or where you are in your journey, trust that getting in touch with what you love and what you believe is right will get you back on track.

CHAPTER 3
Home In on Your Target

"Don't set your goals too low. If you don't need much, you won't become much."

—Jim Rohn

Life started to change for me by 2006. I had gotten married to Stephanie three years earlier and we had two daughters—Aidyn and Ella. With three children and a wife, my why was stronger than ever. I had also experienced some success in the mortgage industry and wanted to take my business to the next level. I knew that I could become one of the top producers because I just had a knack for it, but I hadn't broken through yet. I wanted to learn what else I could be doing to get ahead. Not only did I read every book, but I attended every seminar, conference, and training program that I could. I got to listen to some of the most iconic people in the mortgage business speak, such as Barry Habib, Todd Duncan, Steven Marshall, and Bill Hart. Many of them have become bestselling authors and still speak to this day. I learned so much at these events that I'd sit there and take pages and pages of notes. I became a self-help junkie and went to listen to people like Tony Robbins speak. I was in awe of how much I was learning, but if there was one lesson that stood out above all of the others, it was the power of goal setting.

Establishing your why is essential because it becomes your source of motivation and drive, but that won't generate results without clear goals. You can be the smartest person on the planet, but if you don't know what you're looking for, how can you ever expect to find it? You can't hit a target that you can't see.

After college, my goals were more like New Year's resolutions. There was no clarity or direction, so after a few weeks or months, I forgot about them because they no longer meant anything to me. Like most people, I had an idea of what I wanted to achieve and do with my life, but I didn't have anything resembling a plan, so those goals never came to fruition. I was determined to change that.

When I returned home from these seminars, my head was filled with so many different ideas that I immediately wanted to start working toward a whole bunch of different goals in all different areas of my life. I was warned countless times not to try and do too much, but I thought that more was better, so I didn't listen. My problem wasn't that I was lazy or not working hard enough. My problem was that I tried to do it all, and despite my intentions, it hurt my productivity. It was paralysis by analysis, and that bled over to my poor staff. It wasn't their fault. They were a capable team, but I was firing so much information at them that their heads were spinning. It was impossible for them to keep track of it all, never mind execute those ideas because they were being pulled in a million different directions. I had to make that same mistake over and over again before that lesson sank in.

I was finally able to break that destructive pattern and come up with a simple, realistic and effective approach to goal setting. I started with that massive list of all the different goals I had in all the different areas of my life, and then I winnowed it down to my top three that I wanted to accomplish in one year's time. Instead of trying to change a dozen things and incorporate a bunch of different techniques and ideas, I focused on three core goals. It became about quality, not quantity, because it's better to be dialed in and 100 percent committed to three things than to approach a dozen ideas with reckless abandon and end up giving a half-assed effort.

Those three yearly goals could be personal, professional, financial, or relationship based. At first, I tried to balance out the three goals in different areas of my life, but any time I tried to achieve that so-called work-life balance, it screwed me up more and I wound up being more off balance than when I started. I think the work-life balance that people love to talk about doesn't exist. It's like a utopia. When are you ever going to have a 10 out of 10 in all areas of your life? Is it even possible to balance your personal and professional lives? At one time or another, one area will take priority. If I'm trying to get ahead in my career, maybe my friendships might take a backseat because that's not as important to me at that time when I'm trying to pay my dues professionally. In fact, any attempt to make those friendships a 10 out of 10 during that time might get in the away of my professional goals, because it would pull my focus. The opposite is true as well. If a family member is sick or in trouble, that will take priority, so I might try to delegate more of my work tasks to focus on what's important to me at that time.

Life is never going to be perfect, and once I stopped trying to make sure all areas of my life were balanced, the happier and more productive I became. You can't do everything all at once, so don't try. Forget about categorizing your goals. Pick the three goals that are most important to you, no matter if they are personal or professional.

EXERCISE

Setting goals is one thing, but coming up with a plan to follow through so you accomplish them is another. Here's a simple plan that allows me to stay on track:

#1. Take each of your three goals and establish where you want to be one year from now.

#2. Break each goal down into four quarterly steps. Where do you need to be at the end of each quarter to hit each of those three yearly goals? Set times to check-in with yourself each quarter to see where you're at and if you're on pace to achieving your goals. Set reminders in your phone if you have to.

#3. Next, break each of those quarterly goals down into weekly steps. This is where you begin to see how realistic your goals are. If they aren't realistic, adjust accordingly, so you can realistically get where you want to be in a year.

#4. Finally, break those weekly steps down into daily tasks. You want to make sure that you're doing something every single day to move toward each of your three goals.

It's important that your goals are yours and that they are realistic. I've always been a super competitive person. It started as a way to prove that I wasn't less than, and that carried over to everything I did. It was almost my way of proving that I belonged in the sandbox. For as long as I can remember, I was constantly looking over my shoulder and trying to be the best at everything I did. I can't deny that attitude got me very far, but it came at a price because I was also setting myself up for failure.

The reality is that there is always going to be someone who is bigger, faster, stronger and more successful than me. I don't have any control over what anyone else does, so if my goal was tied to another person's performance, a large component of that goal was completely out of my hands. More importantly, it had absolutely nothing to do with me. The only thing I could control was working to achieve my own personal best. That's when I learned that it was healthier to readjust my goals and expectations, so that I was only competing with myself.

Once I learned how to set, track, and follow through on achieving realistic goals that I had control over, the results I experienced were nothing short of magic. I realized that by breaking down my big-picture goals into smaller steps that I could actually manifest the results I wanted over a period of time. From that point on, I crushed just about all of the goals I set.

Become the Person Who Achieves Those Goals

What often holds people back and prevents them from achieving their goals is that they don't change. The way you do things now is what got you where you are, so if you want to get some place different, you have act differently and take a different approach. This can be difficult if your goals venture into unknown territory because you don't know what you don't know. There is a simple fix, but few people implement it.

When I started working at the Department of Youth Services, I reached out to the people who were above me to learn their interview techniques. Later, working for the mortgage company out in California, I would take the veteran loan officers out to lunch, even though they were the ones with the money, just so I could pick their brains. They were the people who had already succeeded at what I was trying to do, so it made sense that if I wanted to succeed, I would do what they had done. Simple. It doesn't matter if you're trying to achieve a personal, professional, or relationship goal—become the person who can achieve that goal. That means learning from people who have already achieved it or have gotten to where you want to be. Whatever it is that you want to achieve, someone has done it before, so see how you can capitalize on their experience. You don't have to reinvent the wheel and go it alone. Just ask questions. No matter how successful those other people were, they also encountered resistance and can help you prepare for some of the storms you might not even realize are on the horizon.

As my career progressed, I knew that if I wanted to become a top producer in my field, I needed to see how top producers acted and conducted themselves, so when I left the subprime world and got into my wheelhouse working at Fleet, I had a very simple plan. I looked up all of those top producers in the country, and I called them. A lot of the older guys I worked with at the time laughed at me and thought none of those top producers would ever talk to me. But I had a different attitude. I thought, *Why wouldn't they talk to me?* In fact, I actually expected them to call me back. Not for one second did I think they wouldn't, and guess what? They did!

Was it a self-fulfilling prophecy? Maybe. I do believe in the power of positive thinking, but more than anything else, it was playing to my strengths—in this case, my psych degree. What's the number one thing people like to talk about? Themselves! So, I'd leave these loan officers a message that went something like, "Hey, this is Bill Murphy with Fleet, I wanted to give you a call because I know you're one of the most successful agents and a top producer in the area. I was hoping to pick your brain to see where you thought the market was going and if you had any advice."

Not only was I giving them a chance to discuss their favorite topic, but I identified them as one of the best at what they do—because a little flattery doesn't hurt either. Who hears a voicemail like that and doesn't call you back? To this day, I tell everyone I coach to reach out to those people who are at the level where they want to be. I still do it myself. Just keep in mind that what you have to stop doing can sometimes be just as important as what you should start doing, so this requires being open minded and honest with yourself.

Once I got on the phone with experts, I was a sponge. I tried to take in as much information as I possibly could. And why not? What these people were doing had worked, so I modeled what I did after those who had already succeeded. Of course, some people were assholes. Just because you're good at what you do doesn't mean that you're a good person. So, whenever I spoke with people who I didn't share the same values and ethics with, I was cordial and thanked them for their time, but I didn't take their advice as seriously because it wasn't in line with the person I wanted to become. You want to emulate others who have succeed, but don't compromise your own values in the process.

Create an Implementation Plan

Laying out your goals, reading books, and talking to experts is great, but it means nothing if you don't follow through and take action. I know so many people who are personal development junkies. They read every book, listen to every podcast, and don't miss a chance to see people like Grant Cardone, Darren Hardy, or Tony Robbins speak. They know everything when it comes to goal setting, self-improvement, and being productive. They can tell everyone else how it's supposed to be done, but they can't get out of their own way and their lives never change because their implementation sucks. People can mistake learning for doing. It becomes an excuse, so they don't have to put in the work.

Sometimes getting started is the most difficult part of the process, but there are five key steps you can take at the very beginning to make sure you get out of the starting gate and continually keep your eye on the target day after day:

#1. Declare

If you know that achieving a goal is going to be a challenge, get out in front of that by declaring your goals and making clear the direction you want to go. Tell your friends and family. Focus on people who will encourage you and hold you accountable. That could also involve a coach or a support group. Post it on social media. You want to be humble, and not declare your goals in a way that sounds like you're bragging, but when you let people know what you're trying to do, it accomplishes two things.

First, it gets people on board with what you want to do. If they're good friends, they will try to help you with your goals. Even if that help is just support or words of encouragement, that can go a long way. They will understand your sacrifice and won't stand in the way or put you in compromising positions that make you feel guilty for the time you're dedicating to this new pursuit.

Second, when you make your intentions and goals public, you make it more likely that you will achieve them, because you want to hold yourself accountable. You also want to save face and not have to explain to people that you didn't accomplish what you set out to achieve, so that provides additional internal motivation. If you don't value your integrity and your word, it won't really matter, but if you do value your word, you will want to follow through.

#2. Record

You want to write your goals down and make sure what you read what you wrote down every single day. I have my goals written on my phone, so I can have access to them throughout the day, but you can even take this a step further. Try reading your goals out loud and then recording them on your phone, so you can listen to them every single day. Writing them down is good, but hearing yourself recite them in your own voice takes this up a level. It's uncomfortable at first, because nobody likes hearing their own voice, but that heightens your own awareness, so once you start listening to that every single day, you realize that's your own voice telling you that you can do it. I went so far as to record all of my goals—short term and long term—along with any mantras and motivational statements that I needed to hear at that particular time, and listened to that at the beginning of my run every day. It was only about seven minutes, but that became a part of my routine that not only kept me aware of my goals but helped to make them feel real and achievable in my mind.

#3. Focus

Literally, just think about what it is you want. Believe it or not, that alone will get you far. The reticular activating system in your brain is a network of neurons that home in on what you think about. If you spend your days thinking about buying a brand-new black Mercedes convertible, all you're going to see everywhere you go are black Mercedes convertibles. In other words, you're programming your subconscious, and that is the first step in creating your own reality. Reading or listening to your goals every day will get your mind focused on the task at hand. Thinking about what it is you need to do to achieve those goals will better help you recognize those opportunities when they present themselves. If it's on the brain already, you're more likely to notice it.

#4. Visualize

Start with the end in mind. You know your target, but what is it going to be like when you get there? Take the time to visualize yourself and what will happen when you achieve that goal. Go into detail. How do you plan to celebrate? How will your life change? What will your day look like? How will your career, relationships, or health improve? Try to incorporate all five senses to really help you bring this experience to life. That can include the sun on your face, the feel of the grass, and the smell in the air. Bringing your senses into the mix makes this future feel all the more real and allows you to internalize that positive feeling.

You can do this for your one-year goal, or even during the day when facing a challenge. I've turned visualization into a form of motivation. I learned this after finding myself distracted. Every Tuesday and Thursday at 9:30 a.m. I take a Krav Maga class. Most of the time, I can put aside everything else that's going on and focus, but sometimes I'm thinking of a work crisis or some other storm on the horizon that I will have to fix later. That takes me out of the moment and becomes a distraction. In those situations, I stop and visualize how that event will work itself out. That allows me to stay on my game, remain in the moment, and focus on the class until I can address the problem after. Some days it's harder to do this than others, but by preparing and visualizing my eventual success, I lessen the severity of the storm when it occurs. I believe that visualization is how you get to the next level, but like everything else, you have to truly believe what you're visualizing or it won't manifest.

There have been times when I've incorporated these visualization techniques when listening to the goals I've recorded. It's just an additional way to get you focused on the target, in the right mindset, and convinced that what you want out of life is within your grasp. Once you believe it's possible in your head, it becomes much easier to achieve it in reality, because you've already done it. This is something that I've always done naturally, in some form or another, even when I was young and didn't realize the power of the practice. Looking back, I believe that is the reason why I was so optimistic and always thought that everything was going to be okay.

#5. Do

This is the step that all of those self-help junkies find the most difficult. It's a lot easier to teach and plan that it is to actually "do," but the only way you can create change is to dive in. Stop talking about why you can't achieve your goals or how it's not the right time to get started. You just have to do it. People fantasize about what they want, but very few actually take the steps necessary to accomplish those goals. They plan to start next week, next month, or next year without realizing that the perfect time will never arrive, and the longer you put it off, the less likely that you will actually do it. The perfect time is right now, because those same excuses will follow you forever.

If you're having trouble getting started, try going back and examining your why. That is the key component. You are more likely to achieve any goal when it is directly connected to your why. When I look back over my journal entries over the years, I notice this pattern. Whether you realize it or not, the why is more important than the how. It took me years to figure that out, but if your why is strong enough, the how will work itself out. You will find a way. If your child is trapped in a burning building, you will do everything in your power to save your child. You won't care how. You will just act. That's exactly the way you need to approach your goals. The how will work itself out if the why is strong enough, so whenever you feel that you're stuck on the how, try going back and reexamining the why.

* * *

Sometimes we let our past or other people's opinion define us, and that goes far in shaping our identity. This can cripple our self-esteem, shatter our confidence, and have us placing limitations on what we can accomplish. And when we don't believe in ourselves or think we're capable of achieving more, it's difficult to even start doing something challenging, never mind make it stick and become a habit.

We've all had moments in our past where we let others discourage us from doing something we wanted to do or allowed someone to convince us that we weren't good enough. This is exactly what happened to me after I earned my master's. I considered pursuing my doctorate, but I never did because I didn't think I was smart enough. And where did that come from? Years of being shamed and told that I was less than. I allowed my past feelings of being less than prevent me from even getting started, so I was limiting my own potential. I didn't believe I could do it, and guess what? I didn't do it. Thankfully, I've overcome those limiting beliefs, and have gone on to achieve things I never thought I was capable of before, but to do that I had to get past this first step.

Before you get started, you need to let go of your past and believe that you are capable of achieving more. You need to get your mind on board first. If you're struggling with this step, or if there is even a shred of doubt that you're capable of achieving what you set out to do, make a list of all the things that you have accomplished in your life. Are there moments when you surprised even yourself with what you were able to do? Times when people counted you out, but you proved them wrong?

All too often, we focus on what we don't have, didn't get, or how things could have gone differently. Take a few minutes to really appreciate what you have done. If you're struggling, ask a close friend or a family member to tell you about all of the things you've accomplished or done well. Sometimes we can't see it for ourselves, so their answers might surprise you. Let that sink in. It's so much easier for us to focus on the negative, what didn't go our way, or where we fell short, than it is to focus on what we've accomplished. Remind yourself of what you've done and what you're capable of doing. Use those moments as fuel when you begin to doubt that you're capable of completing a new challenge.

When the Goal Is More Important Than Anything Else

When most people think of Kobe Bryant, they probably think of the five NBA championships, two NBA Finals MVPs, 18 NBA All-Star Game appearances, or the countless highlight-reel moments he provided over the course of his 20-year career. They might even think of his MVP year in 2008 or when he won the Slam Dunk Contest when he first entered the league in 1997.

I'm a huge Celtics fan, and when you are raised a Celtics fan you learn to hate the Lakers, so I couldn't stand Kobe during his career. There was a stretch where the Lakers were one of our biggest rivals, and we played each other in the finals a couple times. For a while, it felt like a revival of the Bird vs. Magic days from the '80s. I have a much greater appreciation for Kobe today, and it has little to do with all of the accolades and accomplishments listed above. It actually traces back to a single moment during the Lakers game against the Golden State Warriors on April 12, 2013.

It was just another game at the end of a long season. The Lakers were fighting to make the last playoff spot in the Western Conference, which would also be their eighth straight trip to the postseason. They were in a dog fight with the Warriors all night. Kobe went down twice in the third quarter—once after hyperextending his knee and again after aggravating an already sprained ankle. But he kept going, and with 3:40 left in the fourth quarter, he hit a three to tie the game at 107. Golden State answered with a bucket, and the next time down the court was, in my mind, one of Kobe Bryant's most impressive moments of his career.

Kobe had the ball at the top of the key. He then made a routine move that he had made countless times before when foul was called on defender Harrison Barnes, and Kobe went down. Kobe was owed two foul shots, but this time he didn't get back up right away. A time-out was called, and eventually, Kobe got up and limped toward the bench. After watching him bounce back earlier that night, and many other times throughout his career, nobody was thinking it was a very serious injury at first, but when he limped back out to the foul line after the time out to shoot two foul shots, it was clear that something was wrong.

What happened, and what Kobe and the Lakers training staff had figured out during the time out, was that he had torn his Achilles tendon. It was a season-ending injury. Talk to anybody who has suffered that injury, and they will tell you that it's almost impossible to walk. Ninety-nine point nine percent of players would have called it a day and headed to the locker room, but Kobe made the decision to shoot the two foul shots—both of which he hit to tie the game back at 109. He couldn't run, so the Lakers immediately had to foul when Golden State inbounded the ball to get Kobe out of the game. As Kobe made his way off the court, he was met with a standing ovation from the fans. The Lakers ended up winning that game by two points.

After the game, Kobe acknowledged that it was a routine play. Nothing out of the ordinary happened, but he felt his ankle pop, almost like he had been kicked. He would later admit that he initially tried to buy himself some time so he could figure out a way to keep playing but was told by trainer Gary Vitti that it would be impossible, so he returned to the locker room after sinking those two foul shots.

Many people questioned how and why Kobe went back out there. He said, "When the game is more important than the injury itself, you don't feel that injury. Not at that time." The example he used was to picture yourself stuck on the couch after injuring your hamstring when a fire breaks out in your house. If your significant other and kids are upstairs, you aren't going to worry about your hamstring when trying to get them safely out of the house, because your family's lives are more important than your hamstring injury.

Most people assume that a competitor as fierce as Kobe never questioned whether he would return, and knew he would always come back, but that wasn't the case. He later admitted that after fielding questions from reporters, he seriously doubted if he could recover from this injury so late in his career. He didn't know if he even wanted to put himself through that because it would be a very long road. He was 34 years old and had already played 17 seasons. Nobody would have blamed him for retiring. But he came face-to-face with his wife and kids in the trainer's room and knew that he had to set an example. So he decided right then that he was going to do whatever it took to make it back on the court the next season. If he was going to retire, it was going to be on his terms.

From that moment forward, there was no turning back. Kobe underwent surgery the next day. He missed the first 19 games of the following season and was back out on the court for the Lakers on December 8, before wrapping up his 20-year NBA career in 2016 with a memorable 60-point performance against the Utah Jazz in his final game. Yes, a player like Kobe Bryant demonstrated toughness, grit, and determination in the face of his own personal storm, but that was all fueled by a strong goal directly connected to his why. Without that why, Kobe may have survived his injury to continue his career—but he would have never excelled for those remaining three years like he did.

CHAPTER 4
Build Up Your Fortress

*"When someone tells me 'no,' it doesn't mean I can't do it,
it simply means I can't do it with them."*
—Karen E. Quinones Miller

Once I started working on myself, I was able to make significant improvements, but I also started to develop tunnel vision, especially when it came to relationships. I would make a lot of the same mistakes over and over again. Whenever I tried to follow Darren Hardy's "Wheel of Life" for goal setting, this area was my one weak link. I used to think that if you had the same interests, you could feed off the other person, but I learned the hard way that that isn't the case. I would probably never admit it at the time, but I was selfish. My marriage to Stephanie fell apart and we divorced in 2009 because I treated our relationship like a business. That was insensitive, shortsighted, and what ultimately tore us apart. Thankfully today we are much better friends and co-parents than we ever were as husband and wife, but it was my fault the marriage deteriorated. I continued to make relationship missteps, but by December 2012, I had grown tired of the same old pattern. I realized that if I wanted something more in a relationship, it was me who had to change.

The first step was figuring out who I wanted to be with— not the specific person, but what kind of qualities. I sat down and wrote out all of the attributes of my dream partner. But relationships are a two-way street, so it wasn't only about what I wanted in another person—it was also about who I needed to become to be with that person. If I was going to manifest this incredible person in my life, I had to become more present and work on my anger issues. I've always had a hard exterior, so I needed to learn how to be more patient, compassionate and understanding. I wrote down where I felt that I needed to be both physically and spiritually to become that kinder and gentler person who was more in tune with other people's needs and desires.

I believe that you get back the energy you put out. Three months later, I met my soulmate online. Not only did we instantly hit it off, but she had every single one of those attributes I wanted in a partner. I had never met anyone who I had so much in common with. What's strange was that even though we had never met, we did cross paths before. Twelve years earlier, we went to the same gym. We were both at that gym on 9/11, gathered around the televisions with everyone else when the second plane hit the World Trade Center. I don't remember seeing her, but we were in the same place at the same time on a day that nobody will ever forget where they were.

On our third date, she joined me on a trip out to California. By the time we returned home, we were both off Match.com, and from that day on we spent most of our time with each other. We did everything together. I never made plans without involving her, and she did the same. There were never any arguments. That was over eight years ago, and still I have never met anyone I have loved and cared about as much as her. I'd go so far as to say the first three years we were together that was as close to a perfect relationship as I've ever had. That all changed on August 13, 2016, and my life hasn't been the same since.

We were at our vacation house in Wakefield, Rhode Island. Nothing seemed out of the ordinary at first. In the morning, we each went out separately for a run. I passed her and her friend on the beach. Everything seemed fine, but a few minutes later, she called me to come pick her up because she was in so much pain that she couldn't walk. I could tell that she was in pain when she got in the car. By the time she reached the ER, she couldn't get out, so I had to carry her inside. She was suffering from repercussions of IBS. At first it seemed minor, but that turned into an overnight stay that was extended to a couple of days. Before any of us had time to wrap our heads around what was happening, she had to undergo surgery.

It was supposed to last six hours. After three and a half hours, the doctor found me in the waiting room. "That's fast!" I said, "Did it go better than expected?" He looked as white as a ghost, and I knew the news wasn't good.

"She perforated on the table and went septic." I couldn't comprehend what he was telling me. "We're going to have to watch her through the night."

There was poison in her body and if it spread to her organs she could die. I phoned her sister and then my mother. I was fighting back tears while on the phone, but as soon as I hung up, I bawled like a baby. I got myself together and, an hour later, I went in to visit her, but I wasn't prepared for what I saw. She was hooked up to a bunch of beeping machines with all kinds of tubes going in and out of her. I was completely devastated.

What followed was a nightmare. She was in and out of different hospitals for 90 out of the next 100 days, but she wasn't getting any better. She had no strength, and when I learned that she had to undergo another emergency surgery, I was scared that if they operated on her again that she was going to die. But they didn't have a choice, because there was a chance that she could go septic again, and that would also threaten her life.

When they wheeled her into the ER, I was disturbed to see the desperate look on the faces of the doctors and nurses. It felt like they thought it was over, so I tried to give them my best Knute Rockne speech to pick them up. I told them how she was one of the strongest and healthiest people that they would ever meet, and there was no doubt in my mind that she would pull through. I don't know if my speech resonated, but I felt better after.

I went back to the waiting room, and seven hours later, I learned that she was out of surgery, but she was far from being out of the woods. They kept her in the hospital for a few more weeks. Her face and features became so swollen that she was unrecognizable, and it wasn't long before she had to undergo another surgery.

Finally, I reached my breaking point. The woman I loved was on her deathbed and there was absolutely nothing I could do about it. I was a nervous wreck. I was at the hospital all day, every day. Sometimes I'd slip out and go over to the TwoTen Oyster Bar where I'd eat sushi and get liquored up before going back to the hospital and falling asleep. I wasn't working out. I had no routine. Work suffered. I felt completely helpless. I was at one of the lowest points in my life, but I knew that I had to be strong if I expected her to be strong, so I tried talking to as many positive people as I could. During a conversation with my personal coach at the time, John Alexandrov, he said something that I will never forget. As I rambled on about the situation and all of these things that were completely out of my control, he calmly asked me, "What's the next best thing you can do right now?"

John had me write a list of all the things that were out of my control. I realized that I could continue to make sure that she received the proper medical care, but I had no control over her condition, and I had to resign myself to that. John then had me write out a list of all the things that were in my control, and to my surprise, that list was much longer. I could control my reaction, and how I carried myself. I could control how I continued to show up as a dad and how I showed up at work. Most importantly, I had control over my mind, because if my mind wandered, uncertainty would creep in, so I could choose to focus on what I could control.

That exercise completely snapped me out of my funk. I realized that there were plenty of things that I could still control. I had a choice. I could sit there feeling powerless and sorry for myself, or I could do the next best thing that I could do to improve the situation. That's when I started working out again. I got back to my routine and would bring my laptop to the hospital. I'd send out emails from the waiting room at two in the morning, but I was getting stuff done. Instead of dwelling on all of the things that could go wrong, and what was out of my control, I focused on what I could control. It wasn't perfect, but it wasn't about being perfect because perfect doesn't exist. It was about racking up small wins and making progress while not allowing the situation to bring me down. That's the secret.

It would be another two years before she completely healed, so during that time I was stuck on this roller coaster ride as she struggled to improve her condition. It was absolutely gut wrenching, but I didn't allow it to bring me down. I may not have slept much, but I worked my ass off. In terms of sales, I had my best year ever, and I even won a courage award from my company at the end of the year. I would have traded it all for this woman I loved to be healthy again, but I learned how to stay the course when storms spiral out of control. That's how you go from surviving in the storm to thriving. Those feelings of frustration, depression, despair, and hopelessness are powerful and will hold you back. You have to feel those feelings so you can process the emotion, but then you have to acknowledge, accept, and get through it, so you can get back on your feet and be headed in the direction you need to go.

EXERCISE

The next time you're feeling overwhelmed, stuck, helpless, or a victim of outside circumstances, take a step back, and break out a pen and paper for this exercise:

Step #1: Write down a list of all the things that are out of your control.
Step #2: Write down a list of all the things that you are currently in control of in the moment.
Step #3: Write down what is giving you the most stress.
Step #4: Write down the next best thing you can do right then.

From that point forward, reframe how you view the situation by not focusing on the things that are out of your control but by focusing on what you do have control over and the next best thing you can do in the moment.

Through that experience, I learned that resilience and the ability to weather these storms don't require willpower. Weathering the storm requires building your fortress. This concept can be difficult for some to grasp because we live in a society of instant gratification, where everyone is in search of a quick fix, but this fortress isn't built in a day; it's built over a lifetime through habits and routines. This fortress isn't going to prevent the storms from arriving. There is no remedy for that, because one of the only guarantees in life is that you will endure storms. What this fortress does is better allow you to not only survive those storms, but to thrive when they occur. These habits and routines reinforce your purpose and bring you closer to achieving your goals, but they also serve as a defense mechanism to keep you on course and prevent you from being swept away or going adrift. They become your anchor.

What works for me might not work for you, but these are some of the habits and routines I've used over the years to build up my fortress. You can use some of these bricks to build your own fortress, but take the time to figure out what works best for you.

What's Your Morning Routine?

You need to hit the ground running right when you wake up, and that means coming up with a morning routine.

I've been getting up early since I was a paperboy. I woke up at the same damn time every morning and ate the same damn peanut butter toast. I'd make sure that I left the house at the exact same time, and I knew that if I ever overslept, even five minutes, that it would be the death of me. At 10 years old, I learned an incredibly important lesson—*never hit snooze!* At the time, I wouldn't be able to tell you what I was doing or why, but on some level, I understood the importance of the little things that helped to condition me over time.

Variations of that routine continued through high school, and later in college. If I didn't go through that routine, I felt exposed and vulnerable, like I was leaving the house without my suit of armor. That routine was what prepared me for whatever storms would cross my path.

If you roll out of bed hating life and feeling miserable about having to go to work, or spend your morning fighting with your kids, your day is off to a bad start. One or two things go south—a bad phone call, or an argument with a co-worker—and you can easily get railroaded. That morning routine is the first layer of bricks in the fortress. You have a lot of options for what to incorporate in your morning routine, but this is what has helped me:

- Journaling: This is something that I only started doing recently, but it's made a huge difference. Today, I take about 20 minutes in the morning to journal, and I do a lot of freestyling depending on what I think I might need to explore. Sometimes I focus on my long-term goals, other times I ask myself questions to get me focused on my goals for the day.
- Meditation: I never believed in meditation, but once I started, it was eye opening because it was so incredibly powerful and helped me remain balanced and grounded. If there is anything that I can attribute to not being an emotional nutcase on some days, it is journaling and meditation. But these things only work if you commit and do them with feeling and passion. It doesn't do you any good if you just go through the motions.
- Reading: This was hard for me at first, but I kept at it and managed to make it a part of my routine. I don't

always have time to actually read, but I've gotten in the habit of listening to audiobooks when I exercise and run. Doing this allows me to go through about two books a week.

- Spirituality: It doesn't have to be religion. Spirituality comes in many forms, but making this a daily practice first thing in the morning can help get you in the right mindset and lift up your spirit.
- Exercise: This can be going to the gym or just walking your dog, but the point is to get you active and your body moving. When you move your body, you just feel better, and the simple act of moving can create the momentum you need to be productive throughout the day. I actually go to the gym right after my morning routine, but it's all working together for the same purpose.

Take as much time as you need in the morning for your routine, and even if you don't have much time, use what you have. If that's only 10 minutes, figure out a routine that you can do in 10 minutes.

Get the idea out of your head that this needs to take a long time. Something I've started doing recently that has become a game-changer takes under a minute. I never used to do this before, but every morning now I make my bed. I learned this after reading the book by William McRaven literally titled *Make Your Bed*. It's so simple, but it helped me declutter both physically and mentally at the start of every day.

Bookend the Day

I may have had a morning routine for as long as I can remember, but I didn't have an evening routine until a few years ago. I avoided it for the longest time because I'm usually fried at the end of the day, but I learned that taking just 15 or 20 minutes makes a world of difference and can help me wind down and prepare for the next day. This routine is always in flux and varies depending on what I might need to work on at any given time, but here are some of the basics I've used to help me wind down at night:

- Cut out distractions: A lot of times people have the TV on in the background, or something that can pull focus from what we're trying to do. Even social media is a major distraction. It may seem harmless, but there is so much drama and gossip going on that it fills our head with crap and takes our attention away from more important things. Social media in moderation is fine, but if you get sucked in, it becomes a complete waste of time, so get to a place mentally where you can focus on the task at hand.

- Avoid the bad stuff: Some people love to watch the news, and this can wreak havoc on your psyche before you go to bed because it's loaded with negativity. Never ever, ever, ever watch the news. Ninety percent of the news stories on any station will be negative. There might be one feel-good story thrown in there, but you're mostly going to hear about heinous crimes, disasters, and everything that's going wrong. Don't fill your mind with negativity right before you go to sleep, because that will set the tone for your night and can carry over into the next morning. It's good to stay informed, but you can look up any information you want the next day. Avoid filling your head with negativity right before you go to sleep.

- Look for positivity. What lifts you up? What puts you in a good mood? Find what you love and try to make it part of your evening routine. That might be spending time with your kids or reading something inspiring and uplifting. It doesn't have to take up a lot of time, but make sure you're doing something you love.

- Avoid stress: Some people take the time to go over their schedule for the next day, and that's what I used to do as well, but I've learned it only stresses me out, so I've cut that out of my evening routine. I now deal with that the following day because that's what works best for me, but if it will put your mind at ease to get your schedule in order and plan the next day, make that a part of your nightly routine.
- Journal: I always take the time to journal about everything that I'm grateful for.
- Check in with yourself. I constantly strive to be better every single day, and I do that by checking in with myself at the end of the day. How did I make a difference? Who did I compliment? How did I contribute? What act of kindness did I perform? What act of kindness did I perform that went unnoticed? What am I grateful for? I take stock of what I did, see how I can be better, and work to make that a part of the next day.

Bookending my day sets me up to handle whatever life throws at me. It makes me feel less stress and anger. That doesn't mean I don't ever get stressed and things always go my way, but when that happens, I don't go home and take it out on my family. I can go home at the end of the day not dwelling on what happened at work. I've learned to compartmentalize, so I can be in the present, and bookending my day is a major reason why.

Figure out what works best for you. You can start by trying out some of these suggestions or incorporate your own. Have patience because not everything is going to be a good fit for you and your life, so take the time to figure out what best allows you to wind down, reassess your day, and prepare for the next day.

If you happen to miss a day, don't beat yourself up. It's going to happen. If all you can do is get your morning and night routines done five days one week, get the five in and feel good about it. That's all that matters. Be proud of it and try to build positive momentum.

EXERCISE

I first learned this from Dan Sullivan but put my own spin on it over the years. While journaling as part of your night routine, write down three wins you experienced that day, and three wins that you want to achieve tomorrow. If you had a bad day without any wins (it happens), write down instead what you learned from the experience, and that will become your win.

What I like to do is reflect on all of those 21 wins at the end of the week and boil them down to the top three. At the end of the month, I take those 12 wins and boil them down to the top three. Keep doing that at the end of the quarter and the year. It may sound pointless, but what you're doing is getting in the habit of something we're going to talk about in a few chapters—focusing on positivity and abundance. This forces you not to look at scarcity and the bad things that might happen, which is easy to do because the brain will always harp on the negative, but to closely examine all of the good things going on in your life. You're programing your brain to think positively. I like to think of it as looking forward by measuring backwards, because this can help set you up for future success.

Forming New Habits

If you go to your local gym regularly, you know there are certain people you can always count on seeing. And when I was living in Worcester, Massachusetts, in the '90s, one of those people was Lou. He was a lawyer, but he might as well have been the mayor of that gym, because he knew everyone and made sure to talk to you when he saw you. I first met him when I was about 16, but when our gym closed down, a group of people went to another gym until that one closed down too, and then we all gravitated toward a third. No matter where we ended up, I could count on bumping into Lou almost every day. He lived for going to the gym. It was to him what a coffee shop or a bar might be to someone else.

Lou's routine was like clockwork. Once he got there, he'd break out the newspaper and ride the stationary bike for a little while. He'd walk around, talk to a few people, and then head over to the Nautilus machines to do a few sets. He never pushed himself all that hard and always seemed to do more socializing than actual working out. After about an hour or two, he'd hit the shower and call it a day. Sometimes he skipped the shower because he didn't break a sweat, but that was his routine and come hell or high water, he stuck to it day after day.

The guy wasn't in bad shape. He was in his 40s at the time, and he was consistent—I have to give him that. He did much more than a lot of people do when it comes to developing a workout routine, but he wasn't improving, and I think he got tired of that. One day, he said to me, "You're in good shape, and you get results. Would you mind if I jump in with you some time, so you can show me some things?"

For the next two weeks, we worked out together. At first, we went at it pretty hard, but after a couple of days, I could tell that his heart wasn't in it. During our second week, he backed out. "This isn't really for me," he said.

Lou went back to his old routine the following week and never asked me again why he wasn't seeing results. Twenty years later, I still see him every so often. We cross paths professionally, and he still looks the exact same, which, on the one hand, is a very good thing. I have no right to judge him. Whatever he wants to do and is comfortable doing is all perfectly fine. He thought of going to the gym as a hobby, and he enjoyed his routine, so more power to him. We all have hobbies, and we don't need to be the absolute best at those things to enjoy them. However, if his goal was to get in better shape, and that was connected to his why, his lack of progress would be a problem. That's when you need to learn how to change your ways and create new habits that stick.

Of course, everyone wants to change and be able to improve, but few are willing to put in the work that's required to change. Why? Because it requires pushing yourself and getting out of your comfort zone to approach things a different way. That's the only way you're going to change. Think about it. Your current thoughts and actions are what led you to this point right now, so unless you start thinking and acting differently, very little is going to change. Keep doing what you're doing now, and you will continue to get the same results.

Creating new habits is difficult, but there are two simple things you can do to help make sure they stick:

#1. Carve Out the Time

Not having enough time is the best excuse in the world, but it's just not true. If you want to do something badly enough, you will find the time. The trick is to make sure you set aside the time for your new habit in advance, so you can't give yourself any excuse. Don't just try to squeeze it in when you can. Put it into your schedule.

Creating a new habit sometimes requires sacrifice, and this is something not everyone adequately prepares for. It could mean less time spent watching TV or going out at night. If the habits you want to implement are health related, it could mean giving up alcohol or junk food. Understand going in that there will be sacrifices and tradeoffs, because if you don't plan for those, you will be fighting an uphill battle and it will be easier for you to give up or revert back to your old ways.

When I decided that I was going to start training for ultra-sports events, I took a lot of grief from my friends for not being around as much. They'd always ask me to go grab a beer after work, and my answer was always the same: "Dude, I can't." I didn't want to tell my friends what I was doing at first because a part of me felt like I was showing off, but I also experienced a tremendous amount of guilt as well. Finally, I decided to simply tell people, "I can't. I have to train." That took away the guilt and made the sacrifice a lot easier for me.

In some cases, sacrifice taken to the extreme can lead to alienation, so it's important that you don't sacrifice so much in the pursuit of your goals that it negatively impacts other areas of your life. I've had this problem with relationships, and after many missteps, I learned that I needed buy-in from my family, friends, and co-workers because they would also be impacted by my sacrifice; otherwise, the sacrifice would cause more problems than it solves.

When I began training for the Ironman in 2019, I went to my family first to make sure they were on board with what I was doing, because that commitment meant that I would have to spend more time training and less time with them. When my fiancée was sick in 2016, I knew that I would be at the hospital and spending more time with her, so I went to my team at work to make sure they wouldn't be caught off guard and to ensure I had their support in stepping away. I also turned to my family to help with my children, dog, and house. Often this just comes down to communication and getting on the same page.

There have been times when there were things that I wanted to do, and I didn't get that buy-in from the people around me, so I knew that it wasn't the right time to pursue that plan. I've learned how important it is to not only get buy-in from those around you but to take their perspective and feelings into account. In the past, I might have tried to hide my intentions, but that was a form of manipulation that only led to problems down the road.

#2. Ease into It

Think about all of the people who make New Year's resolutions to start going to the gym. They buy memberships and hire trainers. That's why gyms are always packed in January. Slowly, those crowds begin to thin out by February, and usually by March everything is back to normal because all those New Year's resolution people have stopped going. What happened? The problem is they shocked their system. They tried to do too much too soon. They weren't prepared to make the change and incorporate that new habit into their lives, so it didn't stick.

If you're trying to create a habit that you know will be a challenge to maintain, the trick is to ease into it. Start slowly. If you're not used to working out or going to the gym, make it a point to go for 10 minutes that first week. That's it. Just get your ass there. Your mind will probably fight you and you're going to make excuses because you don't want to go, but you can convince yourself to go because you know you only have to be there for 10 minutes.

What this does is get you used to creating this new habit slowly, so it's not a shock to your system and doesn't feel like a burden. It's only a small commitment at first, but this is important because habits are built slowly over time. Making small changes today helps you build momentum and change your mindset, so you put yourself in a better position to make the bigger changes down the road. This is a long game you're playing, so don't make the mistake of trying to do too much too soon and burning yourself out. There are two things that are important when trying to establish a new habit:

1. Consistency.
2. Progress.

That's what you want to focus on at first. Make sure you do it every day (or for however many days this particular habit calls for), and make sure you gradually improve. So, that 10 minutes can turn into 30 the next week and 45 the week after that. This allows your body, mind, and schedule to adapt to this new activity and routine. Pretty soon, it will become natural.

You want to do something similar with every challenging habit you're trying to implement. If you want to start getting up at 5:00 a.m. so you can get more done in the morning, but you're used to getting up at 7:30 a.m., it could be a struggle to make that drastic change. You're going to feel exhausted when that alarm goes off at 5:00 a.m. for the first time. You'll probably hit snooze for the first couple of mornings. You might even drag yourself out of bed a couple of the days, but it won't feel good. Sure, you could try to rely on willpower to push through, but you're setting yourself up for disaster. That willpower will eventually deplete, and you'll give up, assuming that getting early just isn't for you. Instead, ease into it. Start by getting up at 7:00, so it's less of a shock to your system. When you get used to that shoot for 6:30 and so on.

The beauty of habits is that they can multiply. For example, if your goal is to start going to the gym, once you can engrain that habit and begin to see progress, it will bleed over into other areas of your life. Suddenly, you're not only going to want to go to the gym, but you're going to want to eat better and improve your nutrition because it will improve your performance at the gym. Then you're going to want to make sure you get enough sleep at night. That one habit, if properly implemented, can lead to a string of other healthy habits.

Set Yourself Up for Success

Habits are habits for a reason, and that's why it's difficult to break bad ones and start good ones. Much of it will come down to you, but there are some outside factors that contribute to your success and failure as well, so you want to make sure you're putting yourself in the best possible position to succeed. With so many things out of our control, you want to focus on three crucial areas of your life that you are 100 percent in control of, and make sure you're doing everything in your power to have them propel you forward, not hold you back.

#1. Surround Yourself with the Right People

If you put a crab in a bucket, it can easily climb out. But when you put a bunch of crabs in the same bucket, no crab will ever get out, because the others won't let it. Crabs will literally pull down any crab that tries to escape. They actually have a name for this. It's called "the Crab Mentality," and it's the perfect illustration of how the people in your life can hold you back.

We've all heard the saying that you are the sum total of the five people you hang around with the most, and I believe there is truth to that. So, who do you spend the most time with? Do you associate with people who inspire you and push you to get where you want to go, or do you hang around with people who hold you back or even discourage you? Believe it or not, all of that rubs off on you and can't help but influence your mindset.

Every once in a while, I'll meet up with my old high school and college friends for a night out or a weekend away. It's good to catch up, talk about old times, and have fun, but I'm also very aware of how I'm in a different place than many of my old friends. They aren't toxic people, but I do know that even though some of them are my very good friends, I have to be careful because we no longer have the same values and goals. If I spend too much time in that world and around those people, it becomes easier to lose sight of what I want and where I'm trying to go.

Where this really gets tricky is when some of those people who don't align with where you want to go are in your family. Every situation is different, and you don't want to cut off family unless it's an abusive relationship that is truly detrimental to your health or well-being, but there is a fine line to walk when it comes to distancing yourself from negative influences. I experienced this often when it comes to the way I push myself athletically and train for various events. I've had people I love voice their concern that I was trying to do too much, and these were family members who had the absolute best intentions and were looking out for my best interest. But what they don't understand is that what they're saying sounds like nails on a chalkboard to me. It's not what I need to hear. I don't want to ever ruin my relationship with any of these family members, so I deal with it one of two ways:

1. I have a conversation with them and try to explain where I'm coming from. Hopefully, I can get them to see things from my point of view and eliminate any potential friction or negativity.

2. If that doesn't work, I limit my exposure. That doesn't mean I cut myself off from the people I care about, but I avoid situations as best I can that might turn negative.

Focus at first on those people closest to you, but realize that negative influences can come from all different areas of your life. Workout partners and colleagues can have a negative influence on you. Once you can recognize that negative influence for what it is, it's sometimes easy to limit it and even remove it from your life.

In the end, you attract what you put out there, and as I've distanced myself from those people who are on a different path, I've attracted those who are either on the same path as me or have already gotten to where I want to be, either athletically, personally, or professionally. Some of the people I'm closest to today are people I've met on various work trips, retreats, and events because we're all in the same boat and headed in the same direction. Our values and goals align. However, it's also important that these people you associate with are honest with you. Just like you don't want to surround yourself with negative people who bring you down, you don't want to be around people who always tell you what you want to hear. It's important to get that healthy, constructive criticism that allows you to grow and become better.

This is an ongoing process that continues to evolve. As I'm looking to enter the next phase of my business, I'm now seeking out those people I hold in high regard who are already doing what I want to do. And during that process, I can't help but grow close to some of those people and have them take on a bigger role in my life both professionally and, in some cases, personally. I can't say that any of my work friends have replaced my childhood friends, but we've achieved a similar level of success, so we relate to each other in a way that I no longer do with some of my friends from back home. It sometimes feels like I'm talking different languages with each group of friends. And I'm not the only one who thinks this. One of my work friends even said, "I can't talk like this when I'm hanging out with my real friends." He does have a point, because I would miss out on having people who truly understand the challenges and obstacles I face if I never gravitated towards people who shared the same goals. I'll go as far as to say that I wouldn't be where I am today had I not done that.

Having good people in your corner who relate to you and understand what you're going through is invaluable because whenever you're stuck, down, or in trouble, one phone call can pick you up and completely change your perspective.

> ## EXERCISE
> Take a closer look at people you spend the most time with. Write down a list of names of the people in your immediate circle. Whether it's two people or 20, take the time to evaluate your relationship to determine if they are in line with where you want to go. What are their goals? Do they align with yours? Is having these people in your inner circle helping or hurting you achieve your goals?

#2. Optimize Your Environment

If your goal is to improve your nutrition so you can lose weight and become healthier, you want to do everything possible to make it easier for you to accomplish that goal. So, if you know that you're prone to snacking on junk food if it's in the house, don't buy junk food and leave it around the house. Instead of forcing yourself to resist the temptation, eliminate the temptation. What often happens is that when you don't give yourself the option, you don't even miss the thing you would normally crave.

If you're trying to get yourself in the habit of going to the gym in the morning but know you have trouble getting yourself moving, prepare the night before. Lay out your gym clothes and everything you need in the evening, so you don't even have to think about it in the morning—you can just go. It makes it easier for you to take action, and it also eliminates any potential excuses you might make in the moment when you have to get moving.

If you want to start journaling, but have trouble getting started, try keeping your journal where you'll see it first thing in the morning, so you have no excuse not to do it. Maybe downloading a journaling app that can give you some guidance will be that nudge in the right direction.

If your goal is dependent on more efficient time management and you find that you're easily distracted throughout the day, or frequently catch yourself looking at your phone, come up with a hack to prevent that. It might be as simple as keeping your phone across the room when you sit down to work, and only allowing yourself to check it at designated times, so you can't pick it up without thinking and begin to aimlessly scroll.

These are all simple steps you can take to begin making your environment more conducive with achieving your goals.

EXERCISE

What is one thing you can change about your environment today?

Look over your goals and consider how something in your environment might be holding you back. Is there a temptation somewhere within your reach that you could easily get rid of? What simple change can you make today to become more productive? Just pick one to implement and work to make it a habit.

#3. Take Responsibility

One of the most common patterns or bad habits that people need to break is making excuses and playing the victim. We've become so good at this that we don't even know we do it, but it's pretty easy to detect when we watch someone else do it.

This became much clearer to me when I stared working in the mortgage business, because very little is as telling about people as running their credit reports and seeing how they spend their money. Some people will come to me and have 25 collections on their account, and a large portion of those people immediately say something like, "Those are not mine." They have excuses for every one of them. It's all about blaming someone else, but what they don't realize is that they will always be in their own way until they figure it out. Often, I just call them out. "It's possible that maybe one or two of these are an error, but do you really think the other 23 are not your fault?" That's not always well received, but we're wasting each other's time if they think otherwise, so it's in our own best interest to not fool each other.

Get in the habit of being honest with yourself. It's our natural inclination to try and pull the wool over our own eyes and coddle ourselves so we feel better, but that will only hold you back. If you turn that instinct on its head and learn to take responsibility (for the good and the bad), you'll be clearing the path so you can grow.

CHAPTER 5
Manage Your Mind

"Don't wait until everything is just right. It will never be perfect. There will always be challenges, obstacles, and less than perfect conditions. So what? Get started now. With each step you take, you will grow stronger and stronger, more and more skilled, more and more self-confident, and more and more successful."

—Mark Victor Hansen

Over the holidays in 2008, I met a bunch of my buddies at Chili's. We were sitting at a high-top table by the bar drinking beers late into the night, when we started joking about running the Boston Marathon. One of my friends had already run it, and suddenly everyone was talking about doing it. They might have been serious at the time, but that wore off by the next morning. However, I made up my mind right then that I was going to do it.

I was 36 at the time, and the longest I had ever run was 10 miles; that had been a decade earlier when I was training to be a cop. I didn't even like to run. Actually, I hated it. But all that mattered was that my friends were telling me that I couldn't do it and that I wasn't giving myself enough time to train. Whenever someone told me that I couldn't do something, that was all I needed to hear. It always gave me the motivation to prove them wrong.

Every year, the Boston Marathon takes place on Patriots' Day in April, which meant that the marathon was only four months away. I didn't have any time to spare, but training wasn't the only hurdle I had to overcome. You can't just show up and expect to run the Boston Marathon. Space is limited. You have to earn your spot. My buddy had been able to get his spot through his father-in-law, who worked for the local police department, but typically, you earn your spot one of two ways. First, you can qualify, which requires running a time in a previous marathon that rivals that of professional runners. There was no way I was going to do that, which meant that I had to qualify the second way, which was to run for a charity.

The very next day, I started researching charities and inquired with Dana Farber Cancer Institute, a prestigious medical institute in Boston, how to run for their team. I had lost a grandfather to esophageal cancer when he was young. He opted to be treated at a local hospital instead of going to a place like Dana Farber, but I always remember thinking that he should have gone to Boston for treatment. That gave me a connection with the cause, but getting one of the limited spots on their team proved challenging. First, I had to fill out an application that included writing an essay about why I chose Dana Farber. After I submitted the application, I had to undergo a series of interviews that were all intended to gauge my level of commitment. Everyone they selected would be representing Dana Farber, so they wanted to make sure they chose people who met a certain standard.

The process got intense, and I was nervous that I wouldn't make the cut. When I asked the guy interviewing me what I could do to increase my chances of being accepted, he said, "You might want to consider increasing your fundraising commitment." As soon as I got off the phone, I reached out to my network to raise as much money as possible. In the last week of January, I learned that I was accepted. For all I know, the only reason I got in was because someone else dropped out, but that didn't matter to me. I was in.

From that point forward, I had one goal: to finish the race. That fundraising commitment gave me even more motivation. It was one thing if I quit on my own, but it would be another if I quit after telling everyone I was going to do it and raised all this money. There was no way I would let that happen, but I still had a very long way to go. Luckily, I had already started training when I made the decision to run and didn't wait around to see if Dana Farber would accept me.

Once I was fully committed and the enormity of what I was trying to accomplish sank in, that's when the mind games began. I was always a gym rat who was in good shape, but I was not mentally or physically prepared to run 26.2 miles. So, I did what everyone does when they need to learn how to do something—I went online. I found a marathon training program on Google Images and then got a book on how to train for a marathon in six months. I just condensed their program down to four months, but there was one more obstacle I had to overcome.

If you haven't been to Boston in January, it's cold. Maybe it was because I was outside for most of that winter, but that year seemed especially brutal. I tried to turn that into motivation to push myself further. On some days, when the windchill dropped below zero, they actually warned us on the news not to spend too much time outside. I immediately thought, *Hell with that! Let's go running!* It was tough at first, but my body adapted. When I came back, my eyelashes and eyebrows were frozen. It looked like I had snow on my head, but that was just my sweat that had turned to ice. It all became just another way to push myself.

What most people don't realize, and what I learned the hard way, is that when you try to run outside during the winter, the cold isn't the only challenge. There's ice, and when snow piles up on the sidewalks, you have to run in the street, and that often means dodging cars. It doesn't matter if I had a flashlight or a reflective vest; I was frequently forced to dive into the snowbanks to avoid getting hit because people couldn't see me—either that, or they had their heads buried in their phones.

I did my research and reached out to as many people as possible, but almost everyone I talked to told me that I wasn't giving myself enough time. They weren't discouraging me; they were trying to warn me about injuries if I pushed myself too hard. I even had to hear it from my mother. "Oh, Billy, you're going to need more time, or you might hurt yourself." Still, I wasn't deterred. All that did was give me more motivation and propel me forward. I still didn't like running any more than I did before, but every time I laced up my sneakers to go outside to train, I thought of those doubters, and that became my fuel. They are what pushed me, and after a couple of weeks, I made a lot of progress.

My endurance increased. I was running more miles every day, and I even adapted to the cold and the snowbanks, but there were some challenges I couldn't have anticipated. My toenails started to bruise, and some even fell off. And when I was out on long runs, my nipples would bleed from the chafing. I know it sounds awful but talk to any marathon or long-distance runners, and they will tell that it's actually pretty common. However, if you haven't ever experienced that before, it's difficult to prepare for, and the pain certainly caught me off guard. I had to learn the hard way that you're supposed to put Vaseline on your toes and bandages on your nipples. As soon as I started doing that, even I had to stop and think: *Oh boy, what the hell did I get myself into?* Through it all, I kept pushing. I continued to do my research so I could learn and get better, but the mind games continued. I may have been taking two steps forward and one step back, but the trick is to focus on the gains and not allow the obstacles to overshadow the progress.

Leading up to the marathon, I consistently increased my mileage and maxed out at 22 miles a day. I would not run the full length of the marathon until the day of the event. A lot of people told me that I wouldn't have to because my body would be prepared if I trained properly and kept up with my nutrition, so I wasn't too worried about that. Still, I was venturing into unknown territory, and there was something uneasy about that.

Those mind games continued right until the morning of the race as I made my way to the village, which is what they called the meeting point at Hopkinton High School, where the tens of thousands of runners gathered. We had to get there no later than 7:30 a.m., but the start times were set in waves, with the wheelchairs going first, followed by the elite runners and so on. I wasn't scheduled to start until about 10:30 a.m., so I had no choice but to hang out. Tents were set up everywhere, and there were a ton of porta potties, yet the lines were still huge. Even after waiting in that long line, I still had a lot of waiting around to do, and that was hard for me to sit there with nothing to do but think about the race ahead. It was even harder when I saw that I was surrounded by professional runners. Not only did they have numbers, which meant that they qualified, but they were applying Vaseline and all of these gels to their body. It was clearly a ritual that I knew absolutely nothing about, so it felt like I had to do the same thing just to make it seem like I belonged.

My anxiety continued to mount until it was my turn to go. I made the three-quarter of a mile walk down to the starting line with the rest of the group, and once the race started, all of that anxiety and the feeling that I was out of my league went away as my preparation kicked in.

Running the Boston Marathon for the first time was a wild experience. You run through the entire city and all of the different college towns, so there were people lining the street almost the entire time from start to finish. There were some memorable stops along the way. At around mile 15, you pass through Wellesley College, which is an all-girls school. They were out on the side of the road with their "kiss me" signs up, so a bunch of guys ran over in that direction.

After running through Boston College, Boston University, Kenmore Square, and Copley Square, the crowd got denser and louder. I knew I was getting close to the finish line, and then I rounded the corner and could see it in the distance.

If you're a professional athlete, you're used to being out on the field and having thousands of people cheering for you. What's unique about running the marathon is that nonprofessional athletes get to experience what that's like as well because, along that 26-mile route, you have thousands upon thousands of people cheering for you. They don't know who you are, and they don't care, but the energy you get from those strangers can't help but lift you up and give you a jolt of adrenaline. Whatever pain you might be feeling at that time all goes away. It's like they're temporarily healing you that with their encouragement, enthusiasm, and energy. I'll never forget the first time I experienced that feeling. It seemed like I was floating—like the crowd picked me up and carried me on their shoulders toward that finish line. Without a doubt, that last mile was much easier than the first.

After four hours and 20 minutes, I crossed the finish line and felt instant euphoria. I had completed my first marathon. And I did so after training for only four months—something that almost every person I talked to said was impossible.

For the next couple of days, I was sore as hell—much sorer than when I was running 22 miles during training. It wasn't the extra four miles during the marathon that made the difference. During the actual event, I pushed myself, and my adrenaline was so high that it masked a lot of ailments. Adrenaline allows you to do things that you didn't think you were capable of, but your mindset is even more powerful.

It doesn't matter what goal you're trying to accomplish or the challenge you're trying to overcome; your mindset can either be your best friend or your worst enemy. If you can learn how to make it your best friend, it will become your superpower, and you'll thrive in any storm.

How to Harden Your Mindset

Strengthening your mindset isn't only about determination and willpower. It begins long before you ever encounter the storm, and it's something that's built up over time. It's a process. Here are a series of techniques to help ensure you will perform well when facing adversity:

#1. Preparation

Aside from telling me that I didn't have enough time to prepare, the second thing every person I spoke to about the marathon told me was to watch out for Heartbreak Hill—the infamous half-mile incline that begins around the 20-mile mark. It's known for being the downfall of many runners, so I made it a point to be prepared for that and trained by running up incredibly steep hills with that in mind.

For the entire marathon, I made sure to pace myself for when I got to Heartbreak Hill, but when I started going up the incline, it didn't seem like much of an incline at all. *This is it?* I certainly didn't become a world-class marathon runner in only four months. But I had prepared for it so well that it was much easier than I had expected, and I cruised up that final hill. There were a lot of things I had done wrong leading up to and during that first event. I didn't know what I didn't know, so I couldn't adequately prepare for everything. But all of the challenges I *was* able to prepare for, I overcame with ease.

One of the best ways to prepare yourself for any challenge is to practice when your competition isn't. I've learned that from author and motivational speaker Andy Andrews, who had a lot of great parenting lessons, but it's also practiced by icons like Tom Brady, Michael Jordan, and Kobe Bryant, who were notorious for getting to the gym before everyone else. I practiced this myself and tried to instill it in my son when I helped him train for football. We'd get up at 5:00 a.m. before he had to go to school, because that would give him an advantage on all of the other guys that he'd be competing against on game day who were still sleeping.

Preparation is half the battle. It doesn't matter what you're doing; if you make sure to put the time in beforehand, you not only become more aware of the potential obstacles that lie ahead, you can also put yourself in a much better position to overcome them.

#2. Mind, Body, and Spirit Are All Connected

It's a lot harder to manage your mind if the body and spirit aren't healthy. Even if you get to a place where you can get the mind on board, it can only go as far as the body will take it.

Don't make the mistake of overlooking your physical health. If you don't feel good and you aren't eating or exercising, it's going to impact everything you do and make you more susceptible to stress. And when you're stressed, it's difficult to perform at your best, or worse, it's easier to quit. I'm not talking about going out to run marathons, but you want to be active and healthy. You can devour all of the self-development and mindset material out there, but if you're not healthy, you won't make nearly as much progress.

The third part of this equation is the spirit. That means different things to different people, but I consider spirituality as a way to cleanse the mind and the body to help create faith and hope. For me, it's my belief in God. Part of my routine is that I read scripture every day and watch online sermons every week. Praying is part of my spiritual meditation, but I know that it's not for everyone. For some people, their spiritual practice can be meditation, affirmations, yoga, walking, or even a daily workout.

#3. Focus on the Process

You always want to have that target in mind at the end, so you know what you're aiming at, but that can't be all you think about. Whenever I hit a wall when running and know that I have to dig deep, I don't think about how much farther I have to go—I think about the next step. It's not the five miles to the finish line that I have to get to; it's the next landmark. If I'm training and listening to music, it's getting through the next song. If it's during the race, it's about making it to the next water station or to a spot where I know my friends and family members are waiting along the route. That gives me energy and a much smaller goal to hit, so it doesn't feel so daunting.

It doesn't matter if we're talking about running, sports, work, or a personal issue. It's easy to feel overwhelmed when faced with such a monumental task, but when it doesn't seem like there is any possible way to get what you need done, don't focus on the result—focus on the next step. Break that bigger goal down into more tangible mini-goals that you can realistically achieve. You will not only overcome the doubt in your mind, but you will also get further than you ever envisioned possible.

#4. Celebrate Small Wins

There is a trick to focusing on the next step: you have to reward yourself once you get there. It does you no good to get to the next step only to immediately face another mini-obstacle immediately after. You need something to pick you up and give you that jolt, because it's not going to happen on its own.

Once I made it to that next water station during the marathon, I rewarded myself with something as simple as walking for 30 seconds while I took a drink of water. When you focus on the small steps and play the reward game with yourself, it helps to eliminate the burden that comes with the gargantuan and arduous task in front of you. Sometimes all you need to do is congratulate yourself once you accomplish that small step. Whatever it is that does the trick, make sure to celebrate even those tiny victories.

I've always been hard on myself, so this remains a struggle for me, but I now understand how important it is, and I force myself to recognize and appreciate the progress I make, no matter how small.

#5. Know What Motivates You

We all have our quirks, and one of the goofy things I do is talk trash to myself as a way to psych myself up. A few times, I've caught myself doing this out loud, but it's mostly in my head as a way to give myself an added boost of energy to keep going. I just keep telling myself that I'm not a DNF'r, and I'm not going to quit. Even if I have to walk a little bit, I will do what I have to do to keep going, but I won't give up. What kind of games can you play with yourself to keep you moving forward? It could be reminding yourself of your goals, charting your progress, or checking in with an accountability partner. For some people, music can be a big motivator. Reconnecting with stories about people who inspire you and have already accomplished what you're trying to achieve can help propel you forward and keep you moving in the right direction. Find out what motivates you and be prepared to utilize that when you encounter resistance.

#6. Reconnect with Your Why

The mind will always find reasons to quit, and those reasons are going to sound pretty damn good in the moment, when things get tough. There is very little that's as important and impactful as identifying your purpose, because that will provide more fuel and motivation than just about anything else. When you're in the moment, it can be easy to lose sight of the bigger picture, so remind yourself of this when things get tough. During that first marathon, I had my own personal goals and wanted to prove to myself that I could do it, but that only gets you so far. What really ended up fueling me more than I could have ever predicted was the contribution I was making and the awareness I could bring to Dana Farber. Depending on what it is and what you're trying to do, knowing that you're taking steps to accomplish your why can be its own form of reward.

#7. Strengthen Your Stress Muscle

When training with my coach in the pool for the Ironman, he introduced me to a drill that tested me in ways that I hadn't been tested before. If I'm being honest, it was terrifying. I'd get in the deep end of the pool and tie a 15-foot bungee cord around my waist that was attached to the wall. The drill was to swim for a minute straight before getting a ten-second break. When swimming, I couldn't go farther than the bungee would allow, so the trick was to maintain my pace to reduce the resistance. I had to learn this the hard way and expended way more energy than necessary. I'd lose my breath, panic, and start to sink. After 10 rounds of that, I was dead. It took me a couple of attempts to realize that I had to get out of my own head, settle my mind, and just relax. For me to even reach that point, I first had to experience being uncomfortable, and that was what made the drill so beneficial.

Many assume that things like ice baths, cold showers, and fasting have only physical benefits, but these tactics are also an excellent way to harden your mindset. The more you can practice getting comfortable when uncomfortable, the better prepared you will be to deal with the everyday challenges and obstacles life throws your way. That's why I trained in the extreme cold during the winter and the heat during the summer. I leave my pool open until November, and even though the temperature of the water can get down to 50 degrees, I still make a point to jump in a few times a week. It's great for inflammation and muscle recovery, but it's the mental toughness it builds that I find the most valuable. It's the same thing whenever I fast for 36 or 48 hours.

Schedule the pain. Schedule ways to push yourself harder, either physically or mentally. Start small. If you aren't used to fasting but want to make it a practice that can build up your stress muscle, start by doing it for 12 hours. If you're not used to going to the gym or working out, start by doing it for 15 minutes, and build up on that. If you struggle to make all the phone calls you want to make during the day at work, set a goal to do just 10 more a day. That's it! Build in a reward when you do it, and pretty soon that 10 will become natural and then you can stretch that even further. Just like kids trying to see who can hold their breath the longest underwater, they build up endurance. The point is to keep pushing yourself beyond your limits. It sucks when it's happening, and there is some anxiety that builds up in anticipation, but afterward you feel great, and each time you do it, it's like you're adding another layer to that suit of armor.

#8. Just Breathe

That's it. It's so simple and natural, yet so impactful. Whenever you're feeling stressed, overwhelmed, or in doubt, just take the time to breathe. Take deep breaths, reassess the situation, and figure out how to best deal with it.

One technique that I've found incredibly useful is box breathing. I learned this breathing exercise from Mark Devine, author of *Unbeatable Mind*. I do this exercise when I'm stressed and have made it a part of my routine when I'm in the sauna after my workout. Think of it as a simple four-step process that involves breathing in for four seconds, holding for four seconds, exhaling for four seconds, and then breathing in again for four seconds. The apps Calm and Muse each have several guided breath exercises that I frequently do. Sometimes I only need to do this for five minutes, and I can notice a difference in my mindset. It can help when I'm stressed out by reducing tension. That tension can deplete your energy and your wind, which is why it's so important to breathe and reduce stress during athletic activities. I've done this a few times before sparring during martial arts or swimming when I felt anxiety. It helped me to conserve energy and be more level headed so I could perform better. I've used these same techniques in the workplace and when dealing with my kids. It's also a great way for me to improve my focus when I find myself distracted.

EXERCISE

Think about a challenge that you are currently going through, or one you see looming on the horizon. It might be something you haven't done before or that's forced you out of your comfort zone, so it can seem overwhelming when looking at how far you have to go. This time around, try approaching it a different way by planning ahead. Ask yourself:

- How can you make sure you are as prepared as possible?
- How can you break down the goal or challenge into steps or mini-goals that can prevent you from being overwhelmed?
- How can you reward yourself when you accomplish those steps?
- How can you constantly remind yourself of your why?

These answers are going to be unique to you and your objective, but if you attack any goal or challenge with this mindset, it will help you stay focused and keep your eye on the prize.

Controlling Your Emotions

Nothing ever goes according to plan, but how do you react when something goes wrong? Do you find yourself complaining about the circumstances? Even if you just complain to yourself, that has an impact on your mindset.

This concept is a big one for me, and I've struggled with it throughout my life. There are many times throughout the day when I can fly off the handle, but there is no way to eliminate emotion. We will always experience good emotions and bad emotions, but so much of managing our minds involves not allowing those emotions to hijack our mood and behavior. Building up our fortress through routines is the best line of defense, but sometimes it's not enough. The following two techniques have been just as much if not more beneficial for me over the years than any other habit I've implemented:

#1. Pause Before Acting

My life changed forever in such a positive way when I joined Fairway Mortgage in 2007, and I owe much of my success to CEO Steve Jacobson. He's had such an impact on the culture, and has proven to be a great leader, because he puts himself on the same level as all of his employees. It's not just me saying this—he's loved by his employees and has been recognized within the industry as one of the top CEOs. I've learned so much from him over the years that I could fill a book with that advice alone, but if there was one thing that he taught me that has had the most significant impact on my life, it's how to pause before acting.

Whenever I'd get an email that rubbed me the wrong way, or caused my blood to boil, my initial response was to start fat-finger typing a response to someone and firing it off, only seconds later to be hit with a wave of panic. *Oh my God, I can't believe I just hit send!* Then I'd spend the rest of the day regretting that decision. I feel even worse if it happens over the phone or in person. I don't know how many times I've said something to a customer, co-worker, or family member when I was upset, only to kick myself shortly after.

The reality is that when we're emotional we don't make good decisions, and this can get us in trouble. So, whenever I feel myself getting angry and know that I'm about to lash out, I first take a pause and run through a series of questions to help me calm down and put the situation in perspective.

- Where is this going to get me?
- Will this get me ahead?
- Am I maintaining my professionalism?
- How can I reframe this situation?
- How would I feel if the other person acted this way toward me?

You want to respond and not react. That means taking time to cool off before hitting send on that email. If you feel that you need to get something off your chest, write out the email you want to send in a separate document. Get it all out of your system, but don't send anything until you've had a chance to cool off and put things in perspective.

This works two ways as well. If I ever get a voicemail from someone who is pissed off and angry, I won't call them back right away. I'll give them an hour or so before reaching out. If it's a client, I make sure to let them know that I understand how important their call is and that it's a priority for me, so I will call them back as soon as I am free. That way they understand the urgency of the situation and that I will get back to them, while giving them chance to cool off. When I do speak to them, they might still be upset but are never as angry as they were earlier. It's a very simple way to diffuse a situation.

One trick I've learned that can help me cut my angry reactions off at the pass and insulate my fortress is checking in with myself throughout the day. Sometimes those reactions aren't only based on what just happened in the moment—they can be an accumulation of what's been building up throughout the day. So, I try to be proactive and not wait for the storm to hit. I do that by checking my levels of anger, frustration, hostility, and anxiety throughout the day to make sure that those negative emotions aren't lingering beneath the surface.

For a reactionary person who is tightly wound, high strung, and prone to snap, maintaining my composure is a daily challenge, and it's one I constantly work on.

#2. Stay Grounded

We all have so many different things going on in our lives that it's easy to get distracted. In fact, distraction is probably our default state of mind. How much time do you think you spend mulling over what's happened in the past and worrying about what's going to happen in the future? If you're like me, it's a hell of a lot more than you'd like. It's so difficult to focus on the moment we're in, but if you can find a way to do that, it's almost like a superpower that will make everything you do so much more effective. If you hit the gym and do a bunch of different exercises without paying much attention to what you're doing, it won't be nearly as effective as focusing on every rep and tapping into the mind-muscle connection. Being able to focus on the present moment can also help you keep your feet on the ground and prevent you from flying off the handle when your emotions are hijacked. There are different techniques and ways that people work to stay grounded, but what's helped me is something I never anticipated.

Mark Devine talked about Krav Maga in his book *The Unbeatable Mind*. By 2014, I had been involved in coaching my kids and played in adult league sports, but becoming involved with martial arts had been on my mind for a while. There was a Krav Maga studio close to my house, so I went in and tried it out. From the very first day, I was all in.

Not only did I enjoy the competition involved, but the practice itself grounded me. Sure, some of it involved being able to take out my aggression and lose myself in a routine. It's physical, and you're learning how to fight, but it was also incredibly humbling. I was in my 40s when I started, and I was sparring with guys who were younger, stronger, and much more advanced. I could go in and try to throw a bunch of haymakers, but the experienced black belts were able to remain calm and take me down.

As someone who has struggled with anger issues his entire life, martial arts has taught me how to maintain my composure and stay grounded more than anything else in my life. Through the techniques, the routine, and the discipline, I've been able to learn self-control. Now that I'm a black belt, I'm the one who has to remain in control when sparring with the newer people of a lesser belt. I've learned not to retaliate if I get rattled. It always goes back to the technique.

When you're doing something that requires all of your focus, everything else gets blocked out. Your mind doesn't wander. You don't focus on all the things that went wrong that day or worry about what might happen tomorrow. All you're thinking about is the person in front of you and what you're trying to do. In that moment, absolutely nothing else matters, and that is incredibly liberating. That composure carried over into my day-to-day life. In time, it helped me put things in perspective. Of course, I could still get fired up. Storms can arrive at any time, and that adversity creates a disruption, but unlike when I was younger, it finally felt like I was more in control of my reaction. It's no longer a struggle for me like it once was, and I have martial arts to thank for that.

Martial arts aren't for everyone. Some people manage to stay grounded through surfing. For others, it's meditation or simply walking outside and being in touch with nature. No matter what it is, try to find an activity you enjoy that can keep you focused on the present moment. You'll find that it's a much-needed respite from your wandering mind.

Experience Gives You Confidence

After finishing the Boston Marathon in 2008, I took a week off from working out and thought there was no way in hell that I was ever going to do that again. In my mind, I was one and done. But I didn't swear off running completely. After a few weeks, I started to run three to five miles as part of my weekend workout, because there was something about it that I craved. It wasn't the actual running—it was how I felt after I finished running that was so powerful.

Whether you believe in it or not, I can personally say that there is such a thing as a runner's high. It can occur while biking, hiking, or during any number of activities, but however you achieve it, it's that release of endorphins that can bring you a feeling of joy and even downright euphoria. Sometimes when I'm running, I turn off my headphones, focus solely on running, and get lost in the moment. That is when I get my best ideas. Once I made that connection, I set out to do more running, biking, hiking, walks on the beach—anything I could to achieve that feeling, because once you get those endorphins flowing, it's addictive. I'd then return home with all of these great ideas that I wanted to immediately put in motion.

After feeling the power of that runner's high, I decided that I wanted to run the Boston Marathon again in 2009. Yes, I wanted to run and push myself, but I also wanted to raise more money for Dana Farber. That became a huge driver for me, because I really liked the idea of upping my contribution. I decided to start training in January again, just like I did the previous year, but this time around, everything was different, mostly because I knew what to expect. I had experience, so there weren't nearly as many unknowns. I had a much better gauge on how to properly prepare, and I knew enough to not make the same mistakes.

You can't help but pick up little things along the way. I even got new sneakers. I had always been a Nike guy, but they aren't known for their running shoes. Nobody wears Nike, which is what I noticed when I showed up at the village and saw everyone in Brooks, Saucony, Asics, and New Balance. I hadn't heard of some of those brands, but they made the best running shoes, so I did my research and found better shoes. Something as simple as that can help give you an edge and propel you forward. It all goes into preparation because the better prepared you are, the better your chance of success.

When it came to the actual training, I stuck with what had worked for me the last time. I downloaded the exact same Google Image training program and got to work on January 2. I had already run for Dana Farber in the past and planned to do it again. I still had to go through the application process, but I had proven myself before, so I was accepted. This time, I had a new goal: finish in under four hours. That meant I paid much more attention to my time when I trained and tried to hit certain milestones as I progressed. It was a personal goal, but more than anything else, it was the contribution and the ability to raise money that motivated me this time around. That was my why that propelled me forward when it was freezing cold outside, and I started to wonder why the hell I decided to put myself through this all over again.

When I arrived at the village before the start of the 2009 Boston Marathon, I was used to the spectacle. I was much more at ease and relaxed. I had my phone with me, so I was making work calls and was even more social with some of the other people. Of course, I was still nervous—that never changes, and that feeling of being less than has always crept in on some level, but I knew not to feed into it, so I tried to have a little more fun.

Sure enough, all of those negative feelings went away as soon as I started the race—that was something else experience had prepared me for. My strategy was always the same, and that was to run just a little bit faster than normal, though not so fast out of the gate that I'd run out of gas. I knew not to fear Heartbreak Hill, so I was going to turn it on at the end. During the race, I kept a careful eye on my watch the entire time. I always knew where I was at, and with three miles to go, I found myself way ahead, but that's when my thighs started to cramp. No matter how much you prepare, something can always come up. I had to slow down and hobble toward the end but picked it up and sprinted the last three-tenths of a mile to cross the finish line in three hours, 59 minutes, and 20 seconds. I hit my goal. I finished in under four hours.

What started as a bunch of guys joking over beers at Chili's put me on the path to pushing my limits and doing things that I never thought I was capable of. Today, it's even become a passion. I completed the Boston Marathon in 2008, 2009, 2011, and 2019. I began Krav Maga training in 2014, earned my black belt in 2018, and then, 11 months later, I completed my first Ironman.

I've come a long way over the years with what I've been able to accomplish physically, but I think some of the biggest strides

I've made have been in relation to my mindset. Even when I was younger and getting things done, it wasn't always pretty because my mindset wasn't healthy. On the surface, I may have made things look easy to an outsider, but on the inside, it was messy because my mind was clouded by anger and negativity. It wasn't until I learned how to manage my mindset that everything started to click for me. That's when I realized that I was the one in control, and I could accomplish way more than I ever realized if I prepared and put in the work. That was the missing piece that propelled me further than any physical accomplishment ever could. Completing that first Boston Marathon gave me more confidence in everything I did from that point forward, be it athletically or in my career. I knew that if I was committed and prepared that I could accomplish great things, no matter what limitations anybody else put on me. That was a pivotal moment that helped me to understand that the competition was really with myself, and all that mattered was what I believed I could accomplish.

You Are Capable of More Than You Think

Elite military training is designed to break you. It's devised to teach you how to far exceed the limits you place on yourself, so you can become better prepared to handle whatever life or death scenario you might face during combat. They do that a number of different ways that include sleep deprivation and being forced to brave the harsh elements for an extended period of time. I never served in the military, but when I heard about a technique called running "the Unknown Distance," it stuck with me.

Running is hard. Running for distance is even harder. But running and not having any clue where the finish line is and where you're going to stop is a whole new level of difficult, because it brings uncertainty into the equation. This military training exercise becomes the ultimate test of how to manage your mind, because making it to the eventual end, wherever that may be, has much less to do with endurance and physical attributes as it does with the story that you're telling yourself.

I first learned about the Unknown Distance from Mark Devine, and I have heard author and veteran Sean Parnell talk about it since, but I think it's a great metaphor for everything we're trying to accomplish. It doesn't matter if we're talking about military training, running, making money, or a whole host of other issues; whether we know it or not, we all have a preconceived set of limitations in our head. *I've only gone this far in the past, so it will be difficult for me to get much further.* And since that's the story we tell ourselves subconsciously, it becomes a self-fulfilling prophecy, and we will rarely get any further because we don't believe we can. In reality, it's not because we can't do it; it's because our minds think we can't.

In May of 2021, I was training for an ultramarathon, which is traditionally any race longer than a marathon. This particular race was 30 miles in Texas. During a trip to the doctor for a physical the week before the race, she asked me, "Are you feeling tired?" I had to think about it, but no, I wasn't. I had a slight tear in my hamstring, but I didn't feel tired. That's when she told me that I was anemic, which is basically an iron deficiency. She then said, "If you've been training up to this point and haven't felt fatigued, you should be fine," but it was too late. The damage had been done, because the seed had been planted. Guess what happened when I went back to training? I started to feel fatigued and couldn't get the idea out of my head that anemia was slowing me down. In all of my journal entries during the week leading up to the ultramarathon, I talked about how I was worried about the event because I felt lethargic, and then something hit me. This was all in my head! It was the placebo effect! I didn't feel lethargic or even think about being tired until the doctor asked me about it. I was perfectly fine. Luckily, I was able to get that thought out of my head before the race—only to be met with another mindset challenge when my brain began to play tricks on me as I neared the finish line.

During these races, I can chart my progress on my watch, or by using other markers on the course. That gives me a feel for where I am and how much farther I have to go, so I can pace myself accordingly. There is a clear psychological shift that occurs as you close in on the finish line. That was especially the case during this race down in Texas. The temperature was getting up into the 90s and continued to rise. The track was a six-mile loop through the state forest, and the race was supposed to be 30 miles. I had been keeping my eye on my watch as I neared the finish line, but it quickly became clear that either my math was wrong, or the race was going to be longer than I thought, because when I hit 28 miles, I learned that I didn't have two miles to go—I had four and a half.

I can't imagine running the Unknown Distance, but I've found very few things to be more debilitating than thinking you're nearing the finish line of a 30-mile race only to learn that you actually have two more miles to go. Those were the longest two miles I've ever run in my life.

I finished the race, but what I realized after was that those final two miles would not have been nearly as difficult had I not already thought I was done. It wasn't the physical part that was difficult; it was the mental part. That got me thinking: what if the situation were reversed, and I thought I had two miles to go only to realize that I had miscalculated in the other direction and the race was actually over? Instead of those final two miles being the hardest of the race, they would have been a breeze.

So many of the challenges we face come down to perception and what we perceive to be our limitations, because that story we're subconsciously telling ourselves becomes a self-fulfilling prophecy, whether we realize it or not. So much of success and achievement hinges on whether we get our mind working for us or against us. The choice is yours. Think that you're capable of more and you are!

CHAPTER 6
Identify and Break Your Negative Patterns

"Reflect upon your present blessings—of which every man has many—not on your past misfortunes, of which all men have some."

—Charles Dickens

There is always more to learn and new ways to improve. My training has come a very long way since I first became involved in the world of ultra sports. I've learned a lot about conditioning and also about myself, but I still make missteps every so often. That's perfectly okay. I know my process is never going to be perfect, but the trick is first being able to identify those

mistakes and then course correct. For me, there was no better example of this than what happened after the 2019 Boston
Marathon.

I had already run the Boston Marathon three times, but
this race was different. When I hit mile 15, I cramped up and
struggled to stay on my feet. Never mind finishing the entire 26
miles; it felt like I could drop at any minute, and I couldn't figure out why. The weather was crazy. The temperature bounced
between 40 and 70. It was windy and raining, and then for a
while, the sun would come out—typical New England weather.
But I was used to that. And I had cramped up when running
before, but I had always powered through it. I knew I was in
great shape. I followed my workout plan perfectly. Something
else was going on that I had missed.

I kept thinking about some of the runners I had met only a
few hours earlier, before the start of the race. I talked to one guy
from Canada who had trained multiple days in below-zero tem-
peratures. He had to run in special metal cleats because of the
ice. I talked to another guy who was using this marathon as a
warm-up for a hundred-mile race out in Colorado. Those stories
made me realize that these amazing feats and accomplishments
were more mental than they were physical. Suddenly, a switch
went off in my head, and I made the decision to do something I
had thought impossible only a few hours earlier—complete the
Ironman triathlon before the end of the year. I never considered
that an option before. Those were superathletes, and what they
did was borderline impossible, in my opinion. How anybody
could run a full marathon after swimming 2.4 miles and biking
112 was beyond me. I had never done any swimming or competitive biking, but I was going to figure it out.

I didn't think I was special—far from it. I'm just a normal
guy, but I believe we are all capable of much more than we

realize. I've witnessed it with many of the people I've coached at work. I do sales training, but it always spills over into personal issues. I've had so many people over the years tell me they could never run a 5k, half-marathon, or marathon. Then, I'll work with them, give them a plan, and next thing you know, they're running their first race. So many people say, "I can't," but if they believe in themselves and commit, they can do it. It doesn't matter who you are—it's all about getting your mind right.

First, I had to finish the marathon. I was hurting. I had to walk some stretches of the race, and the rain picked up as I came down the home stretch, but I wouldn't let myself quit. That wasn't an option. I crossed the finish line, and my family was there to greet me, but I didn't feel much like celebrating. I was disappointed and angry at myself for falling short of my expectations.

Most determined people in that situation would take time off after the race to get in a good headspace, train harder, and come back the following year stronger, but I never adhered to conventional wisdom. I just wasn't built like that. When I got home after the marathon, I joined all kinds of forums and online groups to learn as much as I could about the Ironman. The last race of the season that I could do was only six months away down in Florida. If I didn't make that race, I'd have to wait an entire year. That wasn't an option, but six months wasn't a long time to prepare. If I had any chance of pulling this off, I needed a coach. The training schedules I had downloaded off Google Images weren't going to help me anymore.

I must have reached out to two dozen coaches on multiple forums, but nobody wanted to train me. They said that six months wasn't enough time and that I'd get hurt if I tried to do it that fast because my body wouldn't be able to adapt. I needed at least a year. Some of them probably would have taken my money, but I could tell they didn't believe in me. What's funny was that the people who had already done the Ironman, or a half Ironman, were the most discouraging, but that only motivated me more.

Shirley was a massage therapist I had met through one of my networking groups. She was a tough woman—a former firefighter with a military background who had already completed the Ironman, so I went to her for information and advice. She told me, "By the way, I'm a certified coach." She had never trained anyone for an Ironman before, but she was the first person I spoke with who didn't discourage me, probably because she knew me and what made me tick. More than anything else, it was her enthusiasm and the fact that she didn't tell me what I wanted to hear that gave me confidence, so I hired her. She gave me a workout plan, and I got to work immediately.

I saw some improvement, but the biggest benefit didn't come from how I trained. The most important thing I learned from Shirley was how to focus on my nutrition. I always ate clean. I was healthy and stayed away from junk food, so I never paid much attention to specialized nutrition plans because I didn't think I had to. It was ignorance, but also a little bit of arrogance. I always thought I could overcome anything with mental toughness, so I ignored the plans, and even though I didn't realize it at the time, I paid for it. "That's why you cramped up during the marathon," she told me.

Shirley taught me about bonking. That's what it's actually called. I had never heard the term before, but it's what happens when your body runs out of nutrients, and you crash. Your muscles fail, and you can't continue because you have nothing left in the tank. I didn't even realize that my bad habits were bad habits.

I started eating more carbs, mainly because I was training more and losing weight. I paid more attention to my salt levels and the electrolytes I took in. I increased my potassium—two bananas a day instead of one. There was a strategy to it. I knew what to eat and what to take when. I knew what powders and supplements to put in my hydration packs on what training days. I learned from my mistakes, and pretty soon I felt better than I ever did before in my life.

Bonking isn't reserved for only athletic activities. This can happen at work, in our relationships, and throughout the course of our daily lives. Physical and mental fatigue are a part of life, and there are times when we are forced to push through, but we all have our breaking point. If you don't take care of yourself and overexert your mind or body, that can bleed over and impact the way you think, solve problems, and regulate emotions. It can cause unnecessary stress and even mental health issues. Simply by taking breaks, keeping tabs on your nutrition, exercising regularly, getting enough sleep, practicing meditation, breathing exercises, gratitude, and kindness you can alleviate some of that pressure. It's not going to solve all of your problems. You must still take action and perform, but when your mind and body are healthy and in alignment, you put yourself in a better position to succeed by removing unnecessary obstacles that can cause you to bonk at the worst possible time.

Junk Miles

When I began training for the Ironman, I knew that my weakness was swimming. The 2.4-mile swim was the first of three legs I had to prepare for. College was probably the last time I swam laps in the pool, but I joined the YMCA, jumped in the water, and started swimming. Two trips up and down the pool, and I had to get out. I was exhausted and anxious. I could barely breathe. *How the hell am I going to swim 2.4 miles?*

Shirley gave me a bunch of drills to do in the pool, but I was so far behind the eight ball that I didn't even know what she was talking about. And I was too embarrassed to ask, so I just started swimming laps. I could barely make it up and down the pool once without having an anxiety attack, but I stuck with it, and I did manage to make some improvements. I built up endurance in the pool, developed a training routine, and I thought I was doing great. I didn't realize it, but I was actually doing damage.

About six weeks after I started training, I entered the mini-triathlon—my first of three practice events for the Ironman. It was only a half-mile swim, but before I even got in the water, I knew that I was in trouble. Since there are about 300 people in the water at the same time, they stagger the starts. The most experienced go first, the least experienced last, and then there was me. They put me in a category called "friends of triathletes," so I wasn't even grouped with the main athletes competing. To add insult to injury, all of the inexperienced swimmers were given a fluorescent green swim cap so they could easily pick us out if we struggled, needed assistance, or started going down and had to be fished out of the water.

It didn't get any better when the race began. The current whipped me around, and the waves were brutal. Being out in the ocean was much different than swimming laps in the pool. I had to deal with the swells and the wind. It was only a half-mile swim, but by the time I had finished, it felt like five miles. That's when I got worried about the Ironman, because I knew that I wasn't even close to being in the shape I needed to be in, and it all traced back to the bad habits and patterns I had developed when training.

By only swimming laps and not pushing myself or doing the drills, I was just going through the motions. I was stuck in my comfort zone, so I wasn't improving. Sure, I was swimming miles, but those were "junk miles." They weren't getting me ready for the race or the elements that I'd face when out in the ocean. I had been fooling myself without realizing it, but once I became aware of it, and identified my patterns, I had a choice to make. I could keep doing what I was doing and remain in my comfort zone, or I could push myself to get better.

Shirley was invaluable as a coach, but because I needed so much extra help in the pool, I hired Ho to be my swim coach because he had experience coaching triathletes. Immediately, he helped me with my technique and stroke. He made sure I used my feet properly. That made me a more efficient swimmer, so I could swim long distances without getting tired like I used to. I got better and gained some much-needed endurance.

I don't think Ho took me seriously at first, but I was anxious to learn, and I wanted him to tell me what I was doing wrong that was holding me back. I knew that I needed to kick my training into high gear, so I had him work with me on the drills Shirley had given me. Some of the exercises were crazy. Some involved paddles; others had me swimming with one arm. I had to learn how to breathe from both sides instead of just one like I had been doing. I also started swimming a lot of sprints, with little rest time in between sets. I was absolutely gassed but had to push my body to keep going.

Within a week, I noticed a difference in my performance, and the next time I did an ocean swim, it was like night and day compared to my first effort. All of those sprints and techniques got me in swimming shape, so I could deal with the elements without it completely draining my energy and making me anxious. When you're tired and sucking wind, that's when the wheels come off the bus and everything goes wrong. It makes your heart rate go up, which causes you to panic. When that happens, you start to take on water, and before you know it, you're flagging down the lifeguard to pull you out of the water. Those drills helped me reduce my stress levels and remain calm in the water. And it wasn't like I was spending any more time in the pool or swimming any more laps. I just better utilized my time by pushing myself as hard as I possibly could to make the most out of my training.

The concept of junk miles was such a profound realization that I started looking at other areas of my life to see where I might have been phoning it in, and I was shocked to see that this was one reason why my career had plateaued. It had been right there in front of me, and I had never noticed it before. For the previous 10 years, my yearly sales always capped out in the $60-million range. Every year, I had set goals to exceed $70 million, but I kept falling short of that threshold. I was already working 55 to 60 hours a week and really going hard, so a part of me thought maybe I had hit my ceiling, but it all connected back to junk miles. I didn't have to spend more time; I had to better utilize the time that I was spending. In other words, I had to change my patterns and my habits. It wasn't about working longer; it was about working hard and identifying the highest payoff activities. How could I be more efficient on a day-to-day basis? Once I started asking myself those questions, everything changed.

Whenever I caught myself drifting, I had to readjust and focus. The more self-aware you become, the more you can pick up on your patterns and break those old bad habits. But you can't ever expect to change if you first can't identify what you're doing wrong, so becoming aware is half the battle. At the end of that year, I surpassed $70 million in sales, and I have continued to surpass $70 million in sales every year since then.

I've learned that it's often not what we do as much as it is how we do it that needs to be changed. You can have a great morning routine and be really good at scheduling your day, but if you're half-assing some of those activities, you're selling yourself short. How we spend our time determines our level of productivity and whether or not we accomplish our goals.

People are very quick to try and create new habits that can help them achieve their goals, but that's only half the equation. Rarely do people consider the bad habits that are holding them back. This is a two-step process that requires you to first identify the negative patterns and time-wasting activities clogging up your days before replacing them with new habits. It starts by examining your daily schedule.

Bulletproof Your Schedule

Think about all of the different ways we waste time throughout the day. Even when we think we're being productive, we can actually be setting ourselves back and wasting time. The classic example of this is people who spend their entire day putting out fires. We all know these people, and they don't go into the day thinking that they want to put out fires, but that's what they find themselves doing day after day. When you look closely, how urgent are these fires they need to put out? More often than not, these people are busy being busy, not busy being productive and accomplishing the tasks that will get them ahead. Whether they realize it or not, some people use putting out fires as an excuse to not put the work in, because it's easier to do that than what's needed to accomplish those most important tasks.

If you work at an office, you see the people who spend their time at the water cooler and in the hallway gossiping or talking about television or sports. On a small scale—a couple minutes here and there—it's perfectly fine. We all need some form of release. But if you're not paying attention, this can eat up a tremendous amount of time. Yet, these same people are typically the ones who complain that they are drowning in work. Think about how many supersuccessful people you know are busy being busy and spend every day putting out fires. Probably not many if any at all.

We all seem to think that our days are packed from the time we get up to the time we go to bed, and we can barely make room for anything else, but a closer look reveals that's far from the case. This became clear to me during the pandemic, when everyone started talking about all of the shows they were binge-watching. I'm not a TV guy, and I've never been a TV guy. I do watch a lot of sports, so I'm sure someone could flip this around on me, but think about how much time bingeing an entire television series can take. Did you realize that to watch all 73 episodes of *Game of Thrones* will take you over three full days? That's over 73 hours. I have nothing against bingeing television shows. We all need a break sometimes, but think of everything you could do if you had 73 extra hours. How much more productive would you be? What else would you be able to accomplish?

You can do this with anything. You can do it with sports, social media, or any number of other things that occupy your day. So many of these activities just fill our time, but if you can squeeze these time-sucking activities into your day, why can't you find the time to go to the gym, cook good meals, take a class, learn a trade, or work on things that will bring you closer to achieving your goals? Don't believe me? Here's the secret: we all have enough time.

Did you ever realize how much you get done the day before you go on vacation? You just crank out what you need to do. You suddenly become extremely good at prioritizing, and everything you're doing is a high-payoff activity. You don't have time to be a fireman that day, and you get so much more accomplished than you normally do in much less time. It's easy to get lazy, distracted, and slack off when you aren't paying attention, but you've proven that you're capable of being productive when you have to be. Why don't you approach every day with that same mentality and urgency? Chances are that junk miles are holding you back, and you might even be aware of those inefficiencies in your daily routine.

Here is a simple four-step process to cut out those time-wasting activities, make your days more productive, and put yourself in a better position to accomplish your goals:

#1. Determine What Your Time Is Worth

The first thing I ask all of my coaching clients to do is determine what one hour of their time is worth. Start with the amount of money you currently earn, or better yet, the amount that you realistically hope to earn. Let's say that is $100,000. If you work 40 hours a week for 50 weeks out of the year, that comes down to $50 an hour. That's your number. That's what one hour of your time is worth. But are you living up to your earning potential?

If you determine that you are worth $50, is it beneficial for you to spend an hour fixing a paper jam in the copy machine when you can be doing other things, and there are people more qualified to fix the copy machine? That doesn't mean you're above those tasks, and it's not meant to discredit anybody in a certain position, but the whole idea is to get the absolute most out of your time. I see so many people at work throughout the day engaging in tasks that are not the best use of their time.

Think about it this way: say you have work that you could be doing, but you put it off because you feel you have to rake the leaves and do yardwork around the house. If you value your time at $50 an hour, you're actually losing money. You could easily pay someone $25 an hour to do the yard work while you focus on activities that are a better use of your time. You'd be making more money and focusing on what you need to get done.

#2. Scheduling Hacks

Being productive starts with scheduling, and that's coming from someone who admits organizational skills are a weakness of mine. That doesn't mean I ignore it, but I do look for ways to make sure that each day is as efficient as possible, and that I'm not doing anything that could be hurting my productivity.

The way I break down my schedule is to start with my highest-payoff activities. These are sometimes a family event, but during the weekday, they are typically my biggest revenue-generating tasks at work. Where I've seen people make mistakes is in scheduling these events, calls, or meetings back to back to back, so their entire day is packed with their highest payoff activities. On paper, it looks like a great way to be super productive, but in reality, it can set you back because all it takes is for one thing to go wrong, or for some issue to pop up that you have to take care of, and it throws your entire schedule out of whack. All of a sudden, you find yourself behind the eight ball, playing catch-up, and stuck in reaction mode.

Another popular way people organize their schedule is to label all of their activities as red, yellow, or green lights. Your green-light activities are what get you paid, or what I would call your highest-payoff activities. Yellow-light activities are more of a personal goal or something that you're working on for yourself, while red-light activities are a waste of time. You then color coordinate your calendar to better understand how you're spending your time. The ultimate goal is to load up on the green-light activities and remove or delegate the red-light activities.

Make sure you're getting those highest-payoff activities done every day and not wasting time on those red-light activities, because that's how you will truly make the most progress. If you find that you still have too many items left over, it's not a scheduling problem, it's a workload and expectations problem that has to be addressed; otherwise, you're setting yourself up for failure.

#3. Beware of the Drift

It happens to everyone. At various points throughout the day, we lose focus, let things slide, don't remain on task, and, ultimately, aren't being true to our desires and goals because we've let time get away from us and have become sloppy. There is a fine line between taking a break and going down a rabbit hole of distractions. If you get to talking to people at the office or messing around on social media, that five minutes can easily turn to 10, 15, or more. I personally notice this when I start slacking or putting off the things that I don't want to do.

There is another side to this coin, because success can sometimes hinder your progress as well. Sometimes when we experience success, we start to feel content, and that's dangerous because we take our foot off the gas. If we decelerate long enough, it can knock us off track and prevent us from achieving our goals. We all get complacent. It's part of being human, and every once in a while, I catch myself doing this as well. It's being able to identify it and course correct that will shorten the duration of your drift.

#4. Give Yourself a Break

When I first started in the mortgage business, I was low man on the totem pole, so it was my job to leave the office for coffee and lunch runs. Other people hated being a gopher, but I liked it because it gave me a chance to get out of the office and break up the day. Over time, that became a habit, so when I moved up in the ranks and was no longer forced to make coffee runs, I would still get out of the office.

When I'm at the office today, I'll typically eat lunch at my desk, but between 11:30 a.m. and 12:30 p.m., I have to get up and get out. I don't do any work or make any calls during that time. It's only for 10 or 15 minutes, but I get a coffee and then listen to sports talk radio. Even when I'm working at home, I do the same thing. When people offer to get me a coffee, I usually turn them down and opt to do it on my own, just so I can get out. That's been a nonnegotiable part my routine for over 20 years, but I didn't realize the true benefit and how powerful it was until a couple of years ago when people kept telling me that I would always come back from these breaks ready to go. That's when I made that connection.

This is not about being lazy. It's about recharging because nobody can go full steam ahead every day. If you try, sooner or later you're going to run out of steam. You need to recharge your battery, and when you do, you can get back at it with even more energy than you did when you started. Taking a break gives me time to clear my head, decompress, and then get right back at it. And when I do, I'm more focused and I'm in attack mode. Whether it's returning from a run, hike, bike ride, or even a 20-minute break during the workday, I'm not only refreshed and full of energy, but that's when I have some of my best ideas. Getting those endorphins flowing is better than any drug.

Equally as important as breaks is what I like to call "white time." Those are small blocks of time that I can utilize to deal with whatever might come down the pipe throughout the day—and something always comes down the pipe. I never schedule more than two of my highest-payoff activities in a row without some white time in between. And that white time is nonnegotiable, because I've learned that it makes me more productive than if I tried to put my head down and bull-rush my way through the day, trying to get as much done as possible.

Is there a pattern to your workday? The closer you look, you might notice that there are times when you are more productive and in the zone and times when you aren't productive or feel overwhelmed. It's different for everyone, but try to schedule your white time or breaks around those times or activities that are the most difficult or that leave you feeling stressed or overwhelmed. Plan it out in advance. That short break or time away might provide you the release you need to make it through those more difficult tasks.

If I mess up at work, it could impact someone's mortgage rate. I take that seriously, but I can't help but think about doctors, police officers, firefighters, first responders, and people in the military who don't have the luxury of being able to make mistakes. They regularly face life-and-death situations and often have other people's lives in their hands, so there is much less margin for error for them compared to what I do. Whenever I think of that, it motivates me to be just a little bit better.

* * *

Give this a try. Set up your schedule to achieve optimal productivity, and then evaluate your execution. Look closely at how you spend your time. Sure, you blocked off an hour for one of those highest-payoff activities, but did you follow through? Were you productive? How well did you spend that hour? Are you really giving it everything you have? The simple act of auditing your day will help you better identify things you're doing that might be killing your productivity without your even realizing it. And there will always be an area where we can do just a little bit more or be just a little bit better. Sometimes knowing is half the battle because you won't be able to improve if you aren't even aware of where you're deficient. By doing this, I've learned that I run into trouble when I have too many things clogging up my schedule. I get overwhelmed, so I force myself to prioritize or reschedule. If I don't, that begins to affect my productivity, so I have to carefully watch myself, but it's often a daily battle to condense and cut down what I need to do.

Remember that everyone is busy. There are 24 hours in a day, but don't ever forget that we all get the same amount of time. It's the same for you, me, and everyone else. There are no exceptions. If you go into work, you're there for the same amount of time as everyone else, but not everyone is the same when it comes to productivity, because not everyone utilizes their time the same way. How you utilize your time will determine if you get ahead and succeed. If you have an hour and a half left in the day, why not try to get the most out of that hour and a half?

Win the Day

The way we handle the big things can be traced back to the way we handle the small things. What we do every single day prepares us for the bigger storms that we encounter in the future. It's during those everyday moments and challenges when we train ourselves, whether we realize it or not. Unfortunately, too many people are setting themselves up for disaster by creating the bad habit of quitting the day.

What is quitting the day? Simply put, it's when you get overwhelmed, flustered, tired, or just don't want to do something anymore, so you don't. That could mean punching out early, cheating on your diet, not going to the gym, putting things off until tomorrow, spending the rest of the day on the couch, or stopping at the bar on the way home. This is all the more common because we live in a society of instant gratification. Everyone is looking for a quick fix and an immediate form of pleasure, but that mentality flies in the face of the discipline required to stick to the routines you need to develop to change.

What most people don't realize is that quitting the day also compounds the problem. Let's say that over the course of the workday, you're feeling overwhelmed and stressed, so you put off what you have to do, push your calls, and tell yourself, "Screw it, I'm going to start over tomorrow." You're so pissed off that you disconnect from everyone else, but you can never truly disconnect from your problems because they will be there when you return the next day. The only difference is that you're going to be behind the eight ball and forced to play catch-up, which could make you even more stressed out and frustrated than you were the day before.

These moments add up. Let's say that happens once a month. On the surface, that's 12 days a year when you packed it in, but it's never just one day you lose. The next day, when you're forced to play catch-up, also cuts into your productivity. That's 24 days where you're not getting done what you need to get done. In my experience, this can be the difference between success and mediocrity, because when you head down this path, it becomes much harder to achieve your goals.

I'm not preaching perfection, and I'm not talking about never taking a break. We're all human and we're all going to feel bad at some point. The problem is when this becomes a pattern. When you quit the day once, you set a precedent that makes it easier to quit the day again and again and again.

Instead, learn to reset the day. It may seem difficult in the moment, but simply sticking it out and making it through the day is one of the most beneficial things you can do to build up your fortress. You might not have the solution to a particular problem or be able to help the way you want to help, but setbacks are temporary. Quitting is permanent. When stuck or challenged, remain composed and ask yourself, "What is the next best thing I can do right now?" That will allow you to make progress because you can't win the day if you can't win the moment.

Doing something hard that you didn't want to do comes with a sense of accomplishment that makes you feel better about yourself. It's those small victories that allow you to thrive in the storm. And once you can prove to yourself that you can thrive in the smaller storms that pop up throughout the day, you will be better prepared to tackle the bigger storms that are sure to come your way.

Owning the day isn't about willpower—it's really about building your fortress, and your fortress is built one brick at a time in each area of your life, through consistency. It will never prevent the storms, but the stronger you make the foundation of that fortress, the less it can be shaken by the storm and the quicker you will recover. Fight for your future by learning how to win the moment and the day.

EXERCISE

Starbucks and Dunkin Donuts make a similar product, and both are successful, but they each do something very different with their coffee. They get to the same place but take separate paths. The script you follow doesn't have to be universal, it just has to work for you, and you have to be willing to pivot and adjust as you go to adapt with what might not be working or need improvement. Your fortress is your own. When it looks like you might be wavering or drifting off course, stop and take the time to do an assessment. It's as simple as asking yourself three questions:

1. What do I need to keep doing?
2. What do I need to stop doing?
3. What do I need to start doing?

Tap Into Your Core Genius

Achieving goals requires organization, structure, and discipline, but it's not all about willpower. You have tools in your toolbelt that will make this job of achieving your goals so much easier. The problem is that some people don't take the time to identify those tools, so they can never capitalize on the things in life that they are good at, or what I like to call their "core genius."

Your core genius is what helps you get through life's challenges. It's what you love to do. It's what makes you special, and how you differentiate yourself. It's how you provide the best value to those you serve. It's your passion and your strength, and it's unique to you.

In addition to grit and determination, my core genius is resourcefulness. That's what got me ahead as a kid, it's what got me through school, and it's how I thrived in the professional world. Ever since I was young, I always looked for an angle. I knew that I wasn't the most athletic, so when playing football, that meant picking up on the little things. On defense, I noticed the way running backs would stare at the hole they were going to hit when they lined up; the way a receiver ran up to the line of scrimmage when he knew he was going to be the target; or the way the quarterback said the plays just a little too loudly in the opposing huddle. That's how I got an edge, but I didn't just look for an angle in sports.

I never had book smarts, but I managed to develop street smarts. When I got to college, I knew that I would have to rely on those street smarts to make it because I felt in over my head. My first two years were abysmal. My GPA was under 2.0, so I needed an angle. I looked around and saw that most of the students in psych classes were women. Some of the classes, like Psychology of Women, were practically all women. So I joined study groups with those women. Instead of getting together with my friends who were either in the same boat as me or didn't care about their grades all that much, I worked with study partners who could help me improve. Not to stereotype, but most of the girls back then were way better students than the guys—at least the guys I hung out with. Being in those study groups helped me learn more, and it took much of the burden off my shoulders, because I wasn't in it alone. Then, when it came time to take electives, I focused on the classes that I knew I would be good at and could easily get an A in—like fitness or motivation classes. That's how I got that 2.0 up to a 3.0 by the time I graduated.

The class sizes were smaller when I got to grad school, and there wasn't the same group setting, so I sought out the professors during their office hours and asked for additional help, just to make sure that I could be as prepared as I possibly could. It doesn't matter what grade you're in, when you ask for help teachers will tell you what to expect on exams and what they're looking for on writing assignments. Teachers are human. If you're hanging on to a 79, simply going to the instructor and asking if there is anything you can do to get that up can sometimes be enough to turn that 79 into an 80. Just trying harder will get you ahead. So many kids never get that, but that was something I learned back in elementary school because I was always looking for those angles at school to make up for what I saw as deficiencies.

EXERCISE

If you haven't already, identify your core genius by asking yourself a series of questions:

- I'm happiest when _____
- I'm most creative when _____
- The activities that make me the most excited to get up in the morning are _____
- I feel like I'm living my purpose when _____
- My hobbies and interests that can generate income are _____
- The talents and attributes I often get complemented on are _____
- The things that I excel at that others struggle with are _____

Once you can identify your core genius, you want to make sure that you're leveraging it. Can you spend 80 percent of your time operating from your core genius? Don't just limit this to work. See if you can expand this across all facets of your life. Go back over your schedule and see how often throughout your day you are utilizing your core genius and how often you are doing something that is not your strength.

If you're firing on all cylinders and at your most efficient, you're leaning into your strengths and delegating your weaknesses. If prospecting, working the phones and dialing for dollars is your strength, but you're not a techie person so you struggle with social media marketing, focus on the phones and see if you can outsource or delegate the marketing. I know that I am not a super organized person, so if someone starts preaching organization to me, I'm going to struggle. That's not my strength. As I've gotten older, I've learned to delegate those tasks and focus instead on what I am good at. The same is true for those red-light activities on your calendar. Delegate those so you can turn your attention to your highest-payoff activities.

It's not easy to grasp at first. I used to think of outsourcing and delegating as dirty words because I didn't want to come off like a dictator. That was something that I just needed to learn to get past because the reality is that all of the best leaders know how to delegate. Today, when it comes to certain details, I trust my team with certain decisions and tasks that aren't the best use of my time because they don't cater to my strengths. This doesn't just apply to work, but what's equally important is how you do it and how you ask for help. As long as you do it tactfully and ethically, you don't have to worry about being manipulative.

You won't be able to delegate and outsource everything, so there is some value in working on your weaknesses. For example, I am not mechanically inclined. I am probably the least handy person I know, but when training for the Ironman, I had to make damn sure that I knew how to change a bike tire because if something went wrong out on the course, I could get stuck in the middle of nowhere and lose valuable time waiting for help. That wasn't my strength, and I didn't want to do it, so I put it off, and when I was training on the bike, guess what happened when I was out on a ride 10 miles away from home? I got a flat tire, but I couldn't change it, so I had to call my son to come pick me up. That night, I went home and watched a bunch of YouTube videos to make sure that I knew how to do it. I even practiced, so that when it happened when training again—this time when I was 80 miles away from home and in a different state—I could change the tire and make it home.

* * *

It can be overwhelming when caught up in the storm, which is why you want to break everything you do down to the lowest common denominator. Go into each day with a plan. By bulletproofing your schedule, you set yourself up to succeed. Not everything will work out as you envision, but if you can lean into your core genius, give your best effort with everything you do to get the most out of your time, and get in the habit of finishing what you start, you will develop the positive habits required to overcome adversity and get you where you want to go.

CHAPTER 7
The Superhuman Power of Positivity

"Nothing can stop the man with the right mental attitude from achieving his goal; nothing on earth can help the man with the wrong mental attitude."

—Thomas Jefferson

When my fiancée got sick in 2016, we had to put our wedding plans on hold. When her condition got worse, we had to push the wedding. It ended up getting pushed three times. We were finally married at the very end of 2017, but she wasn't completely in the clear yet. Her last surgery was in April of 2018. When she was healthy and finally out of the woods, I looked forward to moving on from that ordeal, but what I didn't realize at the time and couldn't have predicted was that our best years were behind us.

My fiancée recovered, but she was never the same after she got sick, and neither was our relationship. Our marriage began deteriorating pretty much from the day it began. There wasn't any one thing that went wrong. It was little things, most of which I didn't even notice at the time, but every day when I look back over the past couple of years, I remember something different, or I see things from a different perspective that allows me to connect the dots leading to the end of our relationship.

This woman was the love of my life. I have never loved anybody as much as I loved her. Even when things were difficult, I always tried to make it work. I went back and looked over all of my old journal entries, and even after the times we argued, I always wrote about how I loved and appreciated her. But in the end, that wasn't enough. We saw a number of therapists, but in May 2020, we briefly separated for five weeks. All the while, I made a conscious effort to save our marriage. Every morning, I told myself that I would fight for our relationship with love, and for a little while, it looked like we were getting back together. As soon as it looked like things were going really well, she would pull away. One afternoon in September, I overheard her on the phone with her best friend, saying, "I feel like I should let Bill go."

I never wanted to get divorced, but that was truly the end of it. I quickly found myself in the middle of the biggest storm of my life—one that I could have never anticipated. I felt completely lost and empty. Very little else seemed to matter. While working out of our vacation home in Rhode Island, I tried to get back on track, but working was difficult, as was keeping up with the habits and routines that had gotten me so far in life. That's when inspiration struck from an unlikely source.

Pistol Pete was another mortgage broker who worked out of Wisconsin. He was an 87-year-old WWII veteran who was still working and doing extremely well. I didn't know him personally, but I definitely knew of him, and he was a fascinating guy. I'd see him at events, and he was on a lot of the company Zoom calls. It was one of those Zoom calls early one morning when, out of the blue, he told everybody that he had been battling cancer. In fact, he had been undergoing chemotherapy for months—all while still working. For the next 10 minutes, he talked about everything he had endured, but never once did he feel sorry for himself. If anything, he had the opposite attitude.

Pete recognized that nobody is immune from tragedy. It doesn't matter how successful you are or how much money you have in the bank, everyone experiences a crisis at some point during their life. It's for that reason he tries to live life to the fullest and take advantage of the time he has with his friends and family. However, the number-one thing he stressed is having a positive attitude. That's why he goes out of his way every day to meet someone he doesn't know, and he always does it with a smile. Pete is a guy who practices what he preaches because when he lost a son a short time later, he continued to stay positive and remains one of the most energetic, caring, loving, and giving people I know.

That day, Pete's outlook on life didn't only strike a chord with me. By the time he was finished, nobody on that Zoom call had a dry eye. In my mind, he was truly a hero. That's when it hit me. I was looking out over the ocean and realized that I had no reason to feel sorry for myself. I had my kids. I had my health. I had my career. Sure, my marriage was falling apart, and that hurt, but my life was still pretty good. In fact, my problems felt minuscule after listening to Pete tell his story. That gave me the kick in the ass that I needed to keep going out there to do what made me happy and accomplish what I needed to get done.

Don't underestimate the power of positivity. Earl Nightingale believed that positivity was the key to all success. In 1956, he recorded *The Strangest Secret*, which is pure motivational gold that still holds up today. It's only about 30 minutes, so every once in a while, I watch it on YouTube. He believed that positivity was the key to all success, and listening to that is always a good reminder for me to focus on all of the good things in my life. It's no joke, because when you are able to remain positive, it not only makes the journey much more rewarding, but it also makes it more likely that you'll achieve your goal. Of course, there will be obstacles, roadblocks, and tough times, but if you truly believe that things will work out in the end and you will be successful, you are more likely to experience success. If you're all doom and gloom and believe in Murphy's Law (no relation), that is more likely to occur.

The classic self-help idea of the power of positive thinking does have science behind it, and it connects to the reticular activating system in the brain. It's not so much that you're manifesting success and positivity as it is perception and that you are opening yourself up to seeing the opportunities you can capitalize on. When you're thinking about something, you are more likely to find it and it's more likely to happen, simply because it's on the brain. Buy a new red car, and you will suddenly see red cars everywhere you go. Why? Because you're thinking about it. Focusing on all the positive things you want in your life won't necessarily make them appear out of the blue, but you are better equipping yourself to see those opportunities when they arise. And when you're negative, you can miss those opportunities because you're too busy focusing on what you lack, which makes it much more difficult to create positivity. Focusing on lack and negativity will only lead to more lack and negativity.

Too many people leave the state of their mind up to chance and let outside factors determine their mood. The problem is that there will always be something that can make us upset or feel bad. It's not easy, but with practice you have the ability to influence your mood, so you can shift from a negative to a positive mindset. From here on out, you can work to take back control and be the one to determine how you feel each day. You have the power to choose the lens through which you see the world. Why not pick a positive one?

EXERCISE

It's natural for your mind to drift to a negative experience or focus on something from the past that you wish happened differently. It could be the end of a relationship or the loss of a job. It could be a time when you were shamed or belittled, or it might be a time when you lost your cool and reacted in a way that you shouldn't have. Whatever it may be, dwelling on bad memories can be debilitating and will hold you back without your realizing it. Think about those things enough, and it becomes a pattern, but it's a pattern you can break.

The next time you have a negative memory, you're going to stop yourself and replace that memory with a positive one. So, when your brain wants to bring you down, you're going to stop and lift yourself up by recalling a time when the opposite occurred. If you're haunted by a memory of a time you were unkind, think of a time when you acted admirably. If you're reliving a memory when you choked, focus on a situation when you performed well under pressure.

It can be difficult to do this right on the spot when you slip into that pattern, so take some time beforehand

(Continued on next page)

to write down those replacement memories you can use the next time this occurs. Visualize that positive memory right down to the smallest detail, and incorporate every single sense, so you can bring it to life in your mind. Think about it almost like you're memorizing a script, so when you slip into that pattern, you can quickly switch gears to think about a victory instead of a defeat.

Changing Your Self-Talk

There have been very few situations in my life that felt more overwhelming than when I arrived at the starting line for the Boston Marathon for the first time. Talk about intimidating. I looked around, and it felt like I was surrounded by pros. These were runners. They talked like runners and acted like runners. I was just a gym rat who showed up with a worn-out pair of Nike's that weren't even really running shoes, but there I was. My mind was going crazy with the self-talk: *I'm in over my head and out of my league. I don't belong here with these people.*

Self-doubt is the fear of failure, and when broken down to its most simple form, is negativity. It's focusing on lack—what you don't have and what you believe that you can't do. It's that voice in your head that is constantly running in the background that continues to reinforce limiting beliefs. And how do you combat anything negative? You flip the script and turn it positive by changing the story you're telling yourself.

Andy Andrews has an excellent quote:

You are where you are because of your thinking. Your thinking dictates your decisions. Decisions are choices. And if decisions are choices and our thinking dictates our decisions, then we're where we are because of our thinking.

This is coming from someone who overcame homelessness and the depths of despair to find success as a bestselling author and motivational speaker. I've gotten to know Andy, and he always speaks about the benefits of positive thinking.

Your thoughts are one of the most powerful weapons in your arsenal, and unfortunately, they are too often being used against you. Negative thoughts can eat away at you. Listen to them long enough, and you can change your mood, kill your confidence, and talk you out of doing what you need to do, but believe it or not, you are the one in control.

The trick is being able to catch your thoughts when they are negative and instantly turn them positive. What makes this difficult is that you can't see your thoughts. They aren't physical objects. Changing your thoughts is much more difficult than building some other habits, but you can plan ahead by creating a mantra. Everyone talks about the power of mantras, but I've found them to be most useful when trying to shift my mindset from negative to positive.

This is my mantra:

Every day and every way I'm getting better and better. I strive to improve my love, health, abundance, riches, contributions, generosity, and philanthropic endeavors, while inspiring others to do the same.

It's changed and evolved over the years. I swap out certain phrases depending on what I might need to hear at that particular time, but I've been saying that to myself for years.

When crafting your own mantra, you want it to contain the following components:

1. It's personal for you, not everyone else.
2. It reminds you of your purpose.
3. It keeps you focused on your goals.
4. It reinforces how far you've come.
5. It gets you excited to make progress.

If your mantra checks all of those boxes, it will help provide that boost of inspiration at a moment's notice while also helping you shift from a negative to a positive mindset. Once you find one that fits, try utilizing it as soon as you wake up in the morning to make sure you're setting the proper tone for your day.

If you're not used to this, it can be difficult at first, so give yourself a little help. Write your mantra on sticky notes and place them around your house, or where you know you'll see them. Put one in a place so you can see it right when you wake up to help set the tone for your day. Make a note in your phone, write it out on an index card that you carry around in your pocket—something that you can easily reference whenever you feel negative. Just like with anything else, if you can do this over and over again, it will become a habit.

You don't only have to rely on a mantra. You can utilize all of the other techniques we've discussed to get you in that positive mindset:

1. Journaling: If you find yourself struggling to get rid of a negative belief, spend time in the morning and or night (whenever, really) rewriting your story the way you want it to unfold.

2. Visualization: Every time you experience self-doubt, picture the positive outcome of the new story you wrote for yourself.
3. Recordings: Tape yourself reading this mantra, or even the entire story, and play it back to yourself whenever you slip into this negative mindset. You can keep it right there on your phone to serve as a reminder whenever you need it.

We can be our own worst enemy and not even know it because we aren't paying attention to any of our self-talk. I've become hyper-aware of this because there are many times when I experience self-doubt.

Once the marathon started, that feeling of self-doubt went away, but I still battle that feeling before almost every event. However, I've since learned how to utilize my self-talk to keep that feeling in check and prevent it from overwhelming me. I follow those same steps. I run through the story I tell myself. I remind myself of my preparation and know that the feeling will go away as soon as that starting gun sounds. I don't focus on anyone else or fall into the trap of comparing myself to others. I focus on myself because that's all I can control, and I know that I will finish because I've always finished. It's gotten to the point now where I've learned how to flip the script and talk myself out of self-doubt by utilizing positive self-talk.

EXERCISE

If you struggle to remain positive, one simple way to begin training yourself is to utilize the alarm on your phone. Set it at three different times throughout the day to go off and

(Continued on next page)

give it the title "think positive." You can call it whatever you want. "Love, happiness, and healing." Whatever gets you to kill your negative thoughts and start thinking positive. Give a name to your alarm that wakes you up in the morning. Utilize Post-it notes and strategically place them around the house in areas where you will randomly see them. This will allow you to reset and focus.

Don't expect to work miracles or to change your mood for the rest of the day. All you're doing is creating a habit, and you do that through a series of one-second shifts from negative to positive. Pretty soon, you'll be able to do it without the reminders, and over time, it becomes more automatic, which means that you're developing a more positive overall mindset.

The Power of Gratitude

We have 60,000 thoughts every day, and 80 percent of those thoughts are negative. It doesn't help that negativity is all around us. Turn on the TV and it's hard not to be bombarded with a constant stream of negativity. If this tells us anything, it's that we have to work to break that pattern.

Negativity comes in a lot of different forms. Shame, anger, frustration, depression, despair, discomfort, and hostility are all low-level emotions that can bring you down, limit your potential, and even prevent you from ever getting started. Sometimes when these emotions take hold, you can't create, and it's difficult to move forward because they are all encompassing. There's a reason for that. Did you realize that it's impossible for anger and happiness to occupy the same space in your mind at the same time? Something's got to give, and you have a say in that. Appreciation, love, and joy will destroy suffering, anxiety, stress, frustration, and worry.

You can't ignore those low-level emotions, or just wait around for them to go away. Do that and they will linger. You have to acknowledge the feeling. If you truly feel it, sometimes the simple act of awareness can take away the power of these low-level emotions, creating room for more positive emotions to enter the brain. However, there is one powerful tool that will allow you to almost immediately replace those debilitating low-level emotions with uplifting and motivating positive emotions, if you can learn to harness it.

As soon as I started learning about personal development, I always heard about gratitude, and I even tried to practice it myself, but I wasn't 100 percent focused or committed, so I didn't get much out of it. Then, one of my first coaches had me do a visualization exercise where I pictured what my life would be like 20 years ahead. I pictured a cookout around the pool in my backyard with my kids and their kids. I used all five of my senses and took in every single sensation and emotion. This particular exercise wasn't specifically about gratitude, but that's what I took from it. I remember feeling so grateful that I had healthy kids and we could all grow old together.

The way I felt after that visualization exercise was like nothing else that I had experienced before and made me truly understand the power of gratitude. My problem was that I wasn't truly embracing that feeling. I was going through the motions and just saying, "Yeah, I'm thankful for my kids and my job..." almost as if I was forced to do it and trying to rush through. It took visualization to get me into that state necessary to truly feel the emotion. By no means is it always easy for me. I'm still very much a work in progress, but I practice gratitude multiple times every day and try to recapture that feeling.

To get started, ask yourself one simple question: What am I grateful for? That's it. It might be your kids, health, family, job, or accomplishments. It's unique to everyone, but really take the time to think about all of the things you're grateful for. For me, it's my kids, our health, my relationships, my career, and my team.

Years ago, I made journaling about gratitude a mandatory part of both my morning and evening routines. At one point, I even had a separate gratitude journal that I kept on my nightstand so that as soon as I woke up, I would grab it and write down everything I was grateful for. Thinking about my kids and all of the things that I'm blessed to have in this world would immediately kill any negative thought pattern and also train me to start thinking more positively. Do that enough, and you'll be able to catch yourself whenever you start thinking negative thoughts or find that your mind is getting bogged down with low-level emotions.

There is nothing I can say about gratitude that will do its power justice. It's something you have to experience yourself to truly understand, so that's what you need to do. Take just five minutes every single day to write down what you're grateful for. Even if you don't believe me, and I know a lot of people don't, just try this out for 30 days. I promise that you will notice a difference and make it a regular habit. You've come this far. What do you have to lose?

Learn to Forgive

If gratitude is one side of the coin, forgiveness is the other. Practicing these skills requires different muscles, and one may come easier to you than another, but they are both absolutely essential if you want to thrive.

Forgiveness can be hard, especially when you feel that you've been wronged. I used to be vindictive and vengeful. We all have at some point. It's part of human nature and growing up, but to remain angry, resentful, and blame others for your situation creates a poison that builds up inside your body and can eat you alive. When you hold onto grudges, you're holding onto what you lack, and when you do that, you can't create. You become stagnant, and all you do is build up more lack. That's how your thoughts can make you sick. This also involves rooting for people to fail. The phrase that always gets me is "karma is a bitch," because that's essentially the same thing. Who are you to root for somebody's downfall? That means you're still thinking vengefully. You're rooting for the negative, and not the greater good.

It can be instinct to react and get mad. You can literally feel the state of your body change, but forgiveness releases those toxins from your body that are causing you harm. Having anger issues for most of my life, I was extremely skeptical of this, so I resisted. Only once I learned how to let go did I realize how heavy the burden was that I was carrying around.

When my marriage was dissolving, I was very upset, and blamed my wife for a lot of what went wrong with our relationship. I tried so hard to make it work, so that was frustrating and got me downright angry at times, but I learned to let it go. If I carried that anger and disgust around with me all the time, it would bring me down and suck all of the positive energy out of my body. It didn't come easy, but now, instead of getting mad, I make a conscious decision to forgive. I do that by looking for the silver linings, and in the case of my most recent divorce, it brought me closer to my kids.

By becoming more self-aware, I've been able to more clearly identify what triggers me. I've learned that I react differently depending on the situation. When competing in the Ironman and having to swim through a school of jellyfish or fix a flat tire on my bike, I can maintain my composure to push through those challenges. Sure, it sucks, but I can remain calm and deal with it. However, I have a much harder time staying composed when someone drops the ball at work or makes a careless mistake. It's in those situations that I react negatively, and it's those situations when I really have to work to check myself. I pause and, before I do anything, I try to put myself in the other person's shoes and see things from their vantage point. But even if I can control my reaction, sometimes that anger can linger and impact my mood, attitude, and ultimately my productivity.

The next technique may sound counterintuitive, but it's proven effective and powerful, especially when dealing with anger and resentment about events that occurred in the past. I send that person blessings. It's nothing I say to them directly or even out loud, but I send them blessings in the form of good vibrations and loving thoughts. One person I do this with is my father. I have plenty of reasons to hold a grudge against him, and a lot of people are surprised that I don't. In the past, I used to ignore him. If he ever reached out to me or asked me for something, I might not respond, or worse, be a jerk about it. Now, I do the opposite and send him blessings. This isn't anything I say to him personally, or even out loud, but I simply wish him the best.

It's easy to be optimistic, positive, active, and enthusiastically pursue your goals when things are going well. It's almost natural, because you're on top of the world, and that feeling can be contagious. What sets people apart is how they act, behave, and think when things aren't going their way. You're never going to eliminate those negative feelings, thoughts, and emotions, but if you change the way you react to that negativity, it will limit how long you are negatively affected. It's not going to happen overnight, and it does require practice, but in time you'll be able to shed those low-level emotions and get yourself into a good place. That's the skill you're trying to hone.

Is there a person in your life who you need to forgive, or who regularly causes you frustration? Instead of indulging in the negative feelings that can eat you alive inside, try taking a different approach and wish them well instead. By staying mad, you're only hurting yourself. Learning how to forgive others and release those negative emotions is one of the greatest gifts you can give yourself. One simple step that will pay dividends in the long run is to work every day on trying to be more positive.

EXERCISE

Try to make it a point to perform just three acts of positivity every single day. That can come in any number of forms:

- Being friendly to someone you don't know.
- Telling someone they did a good job, and truly meaning it.
- Making sure to smile at people.
- Showing happiness for someone else's success.
- Paying a compliment to a total stranger.
- Pointing out the beauty of the view or your surroundings.
- Enjoying the unexpected, even when it's not what you originally wanted.
- Being a source of energy that lifts those around you.

Your attitude determines most of how you experience each day, because you get back what you put out. Once you

(*Continued on next page*)

start exuding positivity and acting like someone who people want to be around, you'll discover that this behavior can be contagious. You might not even realize it, but even by incorporating positivity into a journal practice, you're creating the framework required to make this a positive habit that can replace a bad habit.

Choosing Life or Death

Losing a child is the worst thing that could happen to any parent. I can't imagine having to endure a tragedy of that scale. It makes my own obstacles and challenges pale in comparison. I certainly don't know how well I would cope, and I don't know how I personally would be able to find a silver lining after that loss, but my coach Sarah Middleton has proven that it's possible to thrive in one of the most tumultuous storms any of us could ever endure. And not only has she thrived, but today she's one of the most inspiring people I've ever met and has mastered the art of taking a negative and turning it into a positive.

Sarah and her husband lost their eldest daughter to a drug overdose in 2011. They were shattered and would have done absolutely anything to get their daughter back. It was a desperate time that could have easily left them feeling hopeless, but a message from an elderly pastor set Sarah on her path to healing. He told her, "Every single day, you get to choose what comes into your mind." From that day forward, that's what she did. She turned off all media—no television, newspapers, or radio. An avid reader since she was young, she devoured inspirational books about people who had endured similar loses and learned to thrive. She also became more selective of which people she let into her life. Some of the people around her tried to tell her that she would never recover, but she refused to admit that, so she distanced herself from those individuals. She knew that life would be different without her daughter, and she would miss her for the rest of her life, but every day Sarah made the decision to choose life over death.

Once that decision was made, she became determined to set the positive tone for each day through her morning routine. Setting daily intentions, journaling, reading, and practicing gratitude became daily disciplines. During the day, she made it a point to get active. "Sitting is the new smoking," she says all the time. After learning that our bodies were created to move between 10 and 14 miles a day and that living a sedentary lifestyle can lead to a slew of physical and mental ailments, she made it a point to walk seven to eight miles a day—almost 16,000 steps. Even when on conference calls, she would move around the room to stay active. There was always that hole in her life after her daughter's death, and she knew that life would never be the same without her, but she started to realize how that void was in a strange way directing her to a new purpose.

Sarah had always been a motivated and successful person. She's one of the most successful people I've ever met in my business, but her why began to shift. With so much loss, suffering, and grief in the world, she found her purpose in being the example of how one can emerge from tragedy and become a better person. She chose to do it by helping those who experienced similar tragedies also come out of the darkness and show them that they too can heal. It didn't matter what anyone else had lost or was mourning. It could have been the end of a job or relationship, but she made it a point to be an active listener who always had sympathy for what someone else was going through. She developed a way of being that involved building people up, encouraging and inspiring others, while trying to soothe their pain and add value to their lives whenever possible. She was able to heal by giving back. That today is where she finds her purpose and how she is able to remain positive after experiencing an unthinkable tragedy. I've never met anyone like Sarah Middleton before, and I've learned so much from her in the years that I've known her. Not only is she always positive and optimistic, but I've never once seen her get rattled or lose her composure. She's always in complete control.

Sarah says that in this life, we are either coming out of adversity, living in adversity, or going into adversity, but how we chose to be impacted by that adversity is up to us. Human beings are incredibly resilient creatures, and we all have the capability to emerge from the darkness, but the choice is ours, and it begins with how we chose to show up every day. Do you want to choose life or choose death?

CHAPTER 8
Nobody Can Do It Alone

"Success comes from knowing that you did your best to become the best that you are capable of becoming."
—John Wooden

Almost every day, I am reminded of all the things I don't yet know. I certainly don't have all the answers, and neither do you. There is so much more out there that we can all learn from. That's where a coach becomes invaluable, because that person can teach you and point out things you might not be able to see for yourself.

I tend to think of coaching as an ever evolving and fluid process. I've always eagerly sought out coaching. Whether it was Little League or Pop Warner, I devoured what my coaches had to teach me because I wanted to get better. When my friends would return from summer sports camps, I'd hound them to pass along what they had learned. In school, I looked at teachers the same exact way. So it was natural that when I entered the workforce after graduation, I sought out colleagues, mentors, and experts in my field to tell me what they knew.

Right when my career in the mortgage industry was beginning to take off in 2003, I made the leap and hired my first professional coach. I had been attending conferences and reading books by all of the industry experts, but that one-on-one experience opened my eyes to the real power of many of the concepts I had been hearing about. Of course, I had read about the importance of setting goals, but it was my first coach who got me to fully commit to the process. He was the one who first taught me about tools like visualization and the importance of legacy—things I'm now passionate about. It was almost like that first coach was the bridge I needed between everything I had been learning and how to apply it to my life. That was over 17 years ago, and I have always had a coach ever since.

Today, I'm always looking for ways that I can get an edge, even in the things I'm very good at. I wouldn't have learned about bonking or junk miles had it not been for Shirley. I might have stumbled upon a solution on my own over time by trial and error, but a good coach can jumpstart your process and help you improve more quickly by telling you what to look out for. You may be incredibly prepared and have experience in a certain area, but if there is someone out there who has even more experience, why not learn from them so you don't have to make the same mistakes they did along the way?

Coaching for me has never been a one-way street. The same way that I reached out to others in my industry and learned from the experts who had already accomplished what I was trying to achieve, I enjoyed paying it forward and helping out those who were coming up around me. Before it was ever called coaching, I used to meet with a group of young employees to discuss business and sales. I still love to coach the interns and college kids who work with me, and I find tremendous joy watching them grow into successful businesspeople.

My dad never went to a single one of my games. I saw how my friends had great relationships with their fathers—many of them coached our teams, and I appreciated how they took me under their wing. I always wanted to get better, and I loved to be coached, so when my friends got back from baseball and football camp over the summer, I'd get them to tell me what they learned, so I could use it, too. If it was just a tweak to my swing or a change in my stance, I would take that and go practice on my own. I would have done anything to go with my friends to the football and baseball camps they went to, but my father would never let me go. He would always tell me it was because of money and that we couldn't afford it, but even then, I knew it wasn't true. He had plenty of money to spend on his hunting and fishing trips—he just didn't want to spend the money on me. Because of that, I knew from a very young age that I was going to be involved when my kids started playing sports. That began with coaching my son's T-ball team. When he got older, I helped out with his football and hockey teams. I've coached my daughter's soccer teams, and I didn't even know how many kids were on the field in soccer. When my girls got into cheerleading, there wasn't much I could do there, but I made sure to go to their competitions and be involved any way I could because I never had that, and I remember how I felt when nobody showed up to watch me play. They're going to remember that.

Coaching young kids has its challenges, but it's not always because of the kids. I've built great friendships with some of the parents I've coached over the years, but a small percentage can be super intense and always seem to have an opinion. It's definitely challenging at times, but I've still found coaching kids one of the most rewarding things I've ever experienced in my life. When I can watch a kid learn a new technique or celebrate with the team after a win, very little can compete with that. Not only is it incredibly fun to get wrapped up in the elation of the moment, but it changes my state of mind. It makes me feel positive, and sometimes it really does lift me up and help carry me throughout the day.

Over the years of coaching and being coached, I started to develop my own style and approach. I also got a much better feel for what worked well for me. In 2014, there was a real estate and mortgage coach I worked with who had a proven following and was well respected in that professional community. He was intense and a yeller—the kind of guy who would get up in your face to try and motivate you. I didn't have a problem with that, but during our first week working together, he said, "I don't care about your personal life or what goes on at home. What I care about are your numbers."

He was focused entirely on business, and that didn't quite sit right with me. What if I got into a disagreement with a friend the night before, or something was wrong with my kids? That would change how I showed up and impact my production. That coach was good at what he did, and he had some great podcasts and webinars that were part of his program, so I stuck with him a little longer because of that, but I knew early on that his style wasn't for me.

Whenever I work with someone in a mentoring and coaching capacity, our conversation always goes back to their personal life. It may start out being about the job and the numbers, so we'll talk sales and prospecting, but it almost always goes back to these core principles required for them to work on themselves. That's the key, because if your mind, body, and spirit aren't right, you aren't going to be able to get as much accomplished. When you feel terrible and are having a bad day, it's difficult to be productive. What most people learn is that once you improve the personal, the professional improves right along with it.

I took this same exact approach as I moved into the world of more formal professional coaching in 2017 when my company launched its coaching platform called Ignite. The setting may have been more structured, but I found myself doing the exact same thing I had done when mentoring co-workers years earlier. I always feel the need to check in with people to see how they're feeling and how their mind is before jumping into the numbers and production.

Both coaching and being coached is invaluable. It doesn't matter what you're trying to do, there is always more to learn and always room to improve, but there is only so much you can accomplish on your own. Don't make the mistake of thinking you already have all the answers. There is a world filled with people out there who you can learn from, but before you even go down that road and consider working with a coach, there is one question you need to ask yourself: *Am I coachable?*

For any of this to work, you have to be coachable, which requires you to be open minded in all the different areas of your life. That means you have to be willing to learn, and you have to be willing to take criticism. This can be extremely difficult for some people, especially if they haven't been forced to do it before. The problem is that some people just don't want to change. They either don't want to put in the work or think they know better. When I tried to recommend a couple of books to a new coaching client of mine, he told me, "I don't read."

Apparently, he had never read a book, and he wasn't ready to start. There was pushback on day one, and that reluctance to take advice, get out of his comfort zone, and try a new approach limited his progress. It wasn't much of a surprise when he wasn't able to reach his goals and bowed out of the program.

EXERCISE

You don't need to work with a coach to find out if you're coachable. You can do that right now. The best feedback you can get is from the people you see every day. Turn to your friends, family members, and colleagues because those are the people who will tell it to you like it is. Ask them what they think you are good at and where they think you need improvement. If you're being an asshole, they'll tell you. You can try to fool yourself and say that people don't know what they're talking about, but if you hear the same criticism over and over, that's something you should take into consideration. They might point out some things that are difficult to hear, but you probably need to hear those things to improve.

Accountability

One often-overlooked benefit of working with a coach is that they will hold you accountable. You can have all the best intentions in the world—you can be dedicated, passionate, and want to push yourself—but sometimes it's hard when things get really tough. It's easy to go at your own pace or play mind games with yourself. A good coach will be there to push you further than you push yourself and won't allow you to slack or go at your own pace.

When I hired Ho to train me in the pool for the Ironman, I told him flat out to hold me accountable. I think he wanted to cut me some slack, but I said, "When I'm doing these drills, you can't let me waiver. You can't give me a break. I'm paying you to coach me, so you can't let me slide. The second you see me taking a break or not giving it my all, I want you to be all over me." He might have been a little reluctant at first because he was a swim coach at the YMCA who was used to working with kids. I think I caught him off guard, but when he realized how serious I was, he made sure to stay on me. And it wasn't fun. When those moments arrived, I didn't want to dig down deeper, and if left to my own devices, I probably wouldn't push myself as hard as he pushed me, but that's what I needed to improve. It's not supposed to be fun or easy, but when you're done and have pushed yourself beyond what you thought you were capable of, you can't help but feel great. In my mind, very little compares to that feeling of accomplishment that comes with going beyond your limitations.

I worked with Ho from June all the way up to the start of the Ironman in November, and during that period, I improved exponentially. My confidence was sky high, and by the time I finished my third practice race, I knew that I was ready because I saw how far I had come in the water from when I first started.

Accountability is so important, and it doesn't need to come from a coach. You can turn to a buddy instead. But who you select to hold you accountable is crucial. You don't want to pick a friend who has the same weaknesses as you. If you're both flighty and struggle to get yourselves to the gym, it will be a lot easier to talk yourself out of going and drift from your goal. You won't be good for each other when it comes to holding each other accountable for developing that habit. You want somebody who will hold you accountable no matter what, and that often means finding someone who already has the habit. The added benefit of paying for a coach is that the schedule becomes nonnegotiable.

Take stock of the people around you and see if you have anyone in your life who can serve as an accountability partner to help push you to achieve your goals. It could be a close friend or a co-worker who you know is on a similar path and wants the same things. If so, reach out to that person and see if you can come up with a routine or a plan to help each other out. This can be helpful when trying to create any number of habits that include working out, eating better, being more productive at work, or simply better utilizing your time.

How to Find the Right Coach for You

In my experience, the best coaches never look down on the people they work with—they look at them as equals and peers. It doesn't matter what your accomplishments are or how much money you make; nobody is better than anyone else. That's a healthy mentality to have, but it's not the only quality you want to look for in a coach.

Think of every teacher and coach you've had throughout your life, and you'll quickly realize that they weren't all great. Some were probably awful. Some might have been great for others, but not the best for you. There are a lot of factors to consider when looking for a coach because not only are there good coaches and bad coaches out there, but there are also good coaches who are bad for you. Here is a quick checklist to help you find the right person:

#1. Narrow Your Focus

Right now, I have two professional coaches who help me with very different things. Sarah is a senior VP who has been there and done that—I'm talking about a crazy amount of business that I've never heard of anybody else doing. We talk about once a month, and I find it incredibly beneficial because she speaks the language of our business. I consider that coaching to be more mortgage specific, but we do dip into personal territory, and Sarah does an excellent job of being able to pivot to health and relationship issues when that's what we need to focus on. You should find a coach with the versatility to make that pivot when the situation calls for it.

I also have an executive coach who I turn to discuss more broad-based business concepts. Mike is a brilliant mind who has been a very successful business owner, so I'm always picking his brain. We have a lot of discussions about the bottom line, but we also venture into personal territory and other non-business topics. He's even helped me out tremendously with this book.

Between Sarah and Mike, I learn a lot, and I also get two very different perspectives. They are both veteran experts in their field, but what's great about coaching is that you don't have to turn to someone who is ahead of you in your career. I'd work all day long with some of the millennials in my company to understand more about technology. I know nothing about that stuff. They do, so why would I ever turn down an opportunity to learn from them?

What exactly do you want help or guidance with? If you're looking for a business coach, what kind? Do you want an executive coach or a sales coach? There is a difference. If you're looking to hire a trainer, what are your physical goals? Do you want to lose weight or build muscle? Those are two very different things, and you can find trainers better suited for each goal. If you ultimately want to learn how to work less and earn more, that could be a time management and productivity issue you need help with, so you'd work with a specialist in that area.

What do you need to help you achieve your goals? Get as specific as possible, because that will help you refine your search.

#2. Start with Your Network

If you're looking for a professional coach, start by asking your employer and co-workers to see what resources they have at their disposal. Don't assume that this has to cost you money, or you have to enroll in a formal program. Seek out a colleague or a successful professional in your field and ask them for advice. Ask them if they had any coaches along the way. They might even be willing to coach you or provide you with some invaluable advice.

When I first started at Fleet, I asked one of my managers to teach me who her clients were and how she got them. I was a sponge and took in absolutely everything. Not only did she help me, but she saw my initiative and would later turn over a huge part of her business to me. That wasn't my intention, but just by asking questions, trying to learn, and seeking help from others who were at a level where I wanted to be, I put myself in a better position to reach that level. That proved to be a turning point in my career, and my business took off.

Too few people ask for help, because they assume that successful people don't have the time for them. People want to help other people. Most people don't realize this or think the opposite is true, so they never ask anyone for help. They think that other people are busy, so they don't want to bother them, when in reality, many successful people love to pass along what they know. When in doubt, just ask. Obviously, you have to be nice about it and respect people's time, but you will be shocked by what you can learn simply by asking for advice.

#3. Do Your Homework

Before you work with anyone, and especially before you hire a coach, do your research and learn their credentials. Talk to as many people as possible about the way they work, and then conduct an interview. You have to be on the same wavelength as the person you plan to work with. That means you want to share the same values and have the same basic understanding of your goals. One simple way to do that is to go in with pre-planned questions.

One thing I do with all of the coaches I interview is to start by telling them exactly what it is I want to accomplish and ask them what they think I should focus on to get there. Try this and see what they say, because their answers might surprise you. Don't expect them to lay out a custom step-by-step plan curated to fit your needs, but this is a good way to get a feel for their overall approach and process. You might be surprised by their response (or lack of one), which is why I find this such an incredibly valuable tool when it comes to vetting potential coaches.

I realized how important this was when I became a coach myself and saw that not all clients were a good fit for me or my methods. And guess what? All of that is perfectly fine! It goes to show how important that vetting process is on both sides to make sure you're working with someone who is on the same wavelength and can provide you the guidance in the specific area you need to improve.

Don't be afraid to interview more than one coach. This is encouraged, especially if you're planning on hiring a professional coach for the very first time.

#4. Don't Mistake a Coach for a Therapist

It's a very trendy thing to be a life coach today, and I've watched so many people make the mistake of turning to these so-called life coaches to serve the role that a therapist should serve. There are plenty of people who call themselves life coaches and are phenomenal at what they do, but just like with anything, there are plenty of people out there who don't know what they're talking about. Just because you lived through or experienced X, Y, or Z doesn't necessarily make you an expert on how to deal with the complex psychological issues associated with some of those experiences and conditions.

For me, there is a very clear distinction between a coach and a therapist, and the place where I draw the line is emotion. If you need help working through emotional issues, that's the job of a therapist and not a coach. To consider them the same thing is unfair and downright disrespectful to the doctors and licensed therapists who have put in thousands of hours to learn the techniques and modalities. They have done the research, and many have written on the topics after working with many patients to become experts. There are some excellent life coaches out there who can provide helpful advice when it comes to emotional issues, but you can't look for them to replace trained professionals.

Of course, there are good therapists and bad therapists just like there are good coaches and bad coaches, so you still want to do your homework and always vet the person you're going to hire or work with. Check their credentials, read their reviews, and most importantly, talk to them. I find therapy invaluable, and we can all probably benefit from a little therapy every so often, so don't be afraid to go this route if you identify some emotional issues you want to work on that goes beyond the scope of what a coach can help you with.

#5. Know You Can Switch Coaches at Any Time

Consider this a fluid process of give and take, formal and informal, that will go on indefinitely. Don't assume that just because you begin working with a coach that you've suddenly made a long-term commitment. You have the freedom to change things up when necessary. When something isn't working, or when I've accomplished my goal, I might need to move on to a new coach with a different or more specialized focus. Sometimes you just need a change or a fresh perspective. John Alexandrov was one of the best coaches I ever had, and sometimes we took a break from each other only for me to go back when I needed him again. There are never any hard feelings, at least none that I have experienced. None of this is designed to be a lifetime model. In fact, I'd go so far as to say that you want to change up your coaches, because staying in one lane with one perspective can cause you to get too comfortable. Always look for new ways to challenge yourself, and that often involves changing up your influences.

Utilize Outside Resources

Becoming knowledgeable in something doesn't require you to fork over a lot of money by hiring a coach. There is a world of information right at your fingertips, so if you're strapped for cash and unsure where to start, look for a book. Almost every expert in every field has written a book. When there is something that I want to learn about, before I do anything else, I read up on it. Even before I hired my first coach, I read a bunch of bestselling books on coaching so that I knew what to look for and how to go about doing it.

This wasn't an easy habit for me to develop because I hated to read. I still sometimes find it difficult to sit down and read a book, but since I'm always looking for an angle, I figured out a way to read without actually reading by listening to audiobooks. It quickly became a habit, and then I started listening to books when I trained. Today, I go through about two books a week.

Audiobooks are more popular than ever, but I got in on the trend early. It was my uncle in California who first turned me on to them. He gave me *Think and Grow Rich* by Napoleon Hill and *Awaken the Giant Within* by Tony Robbins. I listened to those tapes every single day on my horrific commute to and from work. He thought they would help me with sales, but it was the personal development aspect that resonated with me the most. Those two books really helped me understand how much more there was to life. I completely wore them out until I literally broke the cassette. I didn't know it at the time, but that would jumpstart my interest in personal development.

Think and Grow Rich was written back in 1937, but it's timeless. Napoleon Hill's story is pretty incredible. He was studying the habits of the most successful people for over 20 years without getting paid. It's still one of the three books that I read every year.

The second is *Rich Dad Poor Dad* by Robert Kiyosaki. It's become one of my favorite books of all time even though I hated it when I first read it. I was still somewhat new to the mortgage industry when I first picked it up, and I disagreed with everything he was saying, so naturally, I thought the book sucked. But as I slowly started to get traction in my business, and learned a little more about real estate, his words started to click. That's when I realized that the dude was right. It was probably my immaturity that made it take me a while to come around to what he was saying, but now I love Robert Kiyosaki. That experience helped me realize how important it is to be open minded when trying to learn something new.

The third book is *The Success Principles* by Jack Canfield. The book's first principle resonates with me the most: "Take 100% responsibility of your life." It's all about responding and not reacting. People often think that we're all dealt a certain hand, so why would you take responsibility for something that wasn't your fault? I learned that perspective from my father, but as I got older, I realized that it wasn't about taking responsibility for what happened to me. It was about taking responsibility for how I reacted to what happened to me. The meaning of this principle changed for me over the years as I came to grips with my past, which is why I think it's so powerful, and why I reread this book every single year.

No matter how many times I revisit these three books, I always pick up on something new. I admit that part of it might be that I miss a lot because I listen when I'm training, but each year I come at the material from a different perspective because I'm in a different place in my life. Sometimes it's like I'm hearing it a different way, and other times it feels like I suddenly understand concepts much better than I did the first time around.

Books are just the beginning. Take to the internet, and you can find a very deep well of resources. One of the most beneficial resources for me is online forums. I wish I had realized this earlier, but online forums are an excellent source of information and motivation. I first discovered the power of these forums when I started training for the Ironman in 2019. There was a forum for people who were trying to train for the Ironman in under a year. I was trying to do it in six months, and a lot of people tried to warn me about potential injuries and told me to be cautious. They didn't have a bad attitude—they were just trying to wake me up to the realities of the situation. I found tremendous value in the information on that forum.

There are thousands of forums out there where you can find people who will encourage you with whatever it is that you want to do. If you're struggling with something, if there is an area of your life where you want to improve, or if you just want to learn something new, then you can probably find a forum dedicated to that pursuit. Just go on there and start asking questions. You will find so many people willing to share their experiences and offer advice. That's invaluable. Even if you don't want to put yourself out there, you can remain anonymous and get the same information. I don't think people explore this option nearly enough. The more people you talk to who have experience doing what you want to do, the more you get a feel for the road ahead and the better you can prepare. And these online forums are where you can meet dozens if not hundreds of such people.

Between forums, books, podcasts, and YouTube, we have more information at our fingertips than ever before, and much of it is free. It's great if you can spend the money to hire a coach, but you don't need to shell out money for any of this if you don't want to.

EXERCISE

Go back over your list of goals and examine them closely to determine how much more knowledgeable you need to become in these areas. How much more do you have to learn? Think about how more knowledge in these areas could put you at an advantage.

Pick one goal (just one), and then pick one way (just one) you're going to seek outside help and advice to achieve that goal. It could be buying a book or joining an online forum. You could watch a series of YouTube videos or listen to an audiobook or podcast on your commute to work. It doesn't matter what it is, but you have to take one step today to learn just a little bit more about what you're trying to do from someone who has that experience.

Digesting Conflicting Information

It is possible to get too much of a good thing.

When I got hooked on personal development, I went overboard and listened to everyone. I was reading books, going to conferences, enrolling in courses, hiring coaches, and getting all of this information from all of these different sources. One day, I read in a book that when you set your goals, it's absolutely imperative to share those goals with as many people as possible to hold yourself accountable and help get people in your corner. Only a few hours later, I was listening to a book on tape that said to keep your goals to yourself and work on them quietly. *Oh, my God!* It felt like my brain was going to turn to mush.

With so much information out there, you can find someone to support just about any idea, and there are plenty of conflicting opinions. So, how do you know who to listen to?

#1. Pay Attention to the Context

When it came to these two ideas related to goals, I'm obviously someone who believes in declaring their goals and making them known. However, over the years, I've come to better understand where that second conflicting opinion was coming from, and it relates back to the crab mentality. If you're surrounded by negative people or naysayers who don't support you and try to pull you down (intentionally or not), it probably makes more sense to keep your goals to yourself. If you declare your goals to these people, and all you hear is, "Why do you want to do that?" "You're crazy!" or "That's a waste of time," what's the point of even bringing it up?

The person giving advice might have a different background or set of experiences that are completely different from your own. People with certain body types benefit from different workout and nutrition plans. Business and sales approaches can differ between your field and location. Everyone's situation is unique, and what works for one person might not work for another, so consider where the person giving the advice is coming from because context matters.

#2. Give It a Shot!

You want to go into this process of self-improvement with an open mind. If you don't, you'll just end up believing you have always believed or remain stuck in your comfort zone, and that won't allow you to change—after all, it's that behavior that got you to where you are today. So, if you come across conflicting advice, and aren't sure which option is best for you, try them both out.

If you're a gym rat like me, think about the first time you ever worked out. It was probably awful. You were sore the next day and didn't want to ever do that again, but you kept going back and eventually saw the benefit. There is always resistance when you try something new. If you can stick it out and push through the resistance, you might learn something new about yourself or find a technique that can change the way you do things for the better. But you will never know for sure unless you try.

#3. Play to Your Strengths

One of the first business coaches I ever had encouraged me to print up 1,000 fliers advertising my services for renovation loans and then go out to Home Depot to hand them out to people in the parking lot. It sounded simple enough, so I took her advice. I made the fliers and drove over to Home Depot, but after 10 minutes, I had enough people telling me to go to hell that I was about to lose it. I couldn't take it anymore, so I threw all the fliers in the trash. And right at that moment, a gust of wind blew in and whipped them up and sent them all flying across the parking lot. The whole thing was a disaster.

She wasn't a bad coach or even giving bad advice—it just wasn't the right advice for me. She was extremely successful, but she was the type of person who could overhear someone talking in the grocery line with someone else about refinancing their home and be able to jump in and close that deal right there in the store. I couldn't do that. I wouldn't feel comfortable doing that because it's not my strength. There are a ton of different ways to do things in our business. There could be four or five core strategies that I implement that someone else who has the same level of success as me doesn't, and vice versa. That doesn't mean that you can't try a different way of doing things, but not every strategy is going to be right for you.

In the end, it all goes back to learning to utilize what you're good at. We all have strengths and weaknesses. We want to continually work to improve our weaknesses but rely on our strengths to get us ahead.

The Meaning of True Leadership

If you've ever had a job in corporate America, you're familiar with reporting to a manager who reports to a regional manager who reports to the senior VP, and so on until you get all the way up to the CEO—but rarely ever communicating with that CEO yourself.

After becoming a rookie top producer my first year working for Fleet Bank, I received a boilerplate email from the CEO of the mortgage lending sector, congratulating me on the accomplishment. I tried to reach out to him but was never able to penetrate the layers upon layers of underlings. My manager tried to tell me not to waste my time, but I didn't understand the culture. I wanted to talk directly to the people who made the decisions and hated the whole approach to hierarchy, but eventually I got used to it. That's the way things were done, and it didn't look like I would be able to do anything to change that.

I had multiple offers when I was looking to leave Fleet in 2007, and I wanted to go somewhere local. Fairway Mortgage was more of an afterthought. CEO Steve "Jake" Jacobson flew me out to the corporate office in Wisconsin for what he called a "Fairway Day," so I could spend some time with the leaders within the company and learn more about the position. Going in, I thought this was going to be all for show, but it wasn't. The company culture was like nothing I had ever experienced before. Everyone I met was genuinely happy and positive, and that started at the top. From day one, I recognized Jake as a different type of leader. He told me, "If we're not a 10 for you in every area, then we aren't a good fit." I thought that would be impossible, but the company checked all my boxes, so that's the job I took.

I've worked at Fairway Mortgage ever since, and I attribute much of my success today to Jake and his leadership style, because it allowed me to thrive in ways that I wouldn't have been able to elsewhere. His style of leadership is horizontal, not from top to bottom. You don't see that often. He'll actually go directly to the salespeople to help make decisions for the company. He would always ask, "Why not us?" whenever we saw the competition doing something or succeeding in ways that we were not, and then look for ways we could achieve that same success.

Fairway has grown from 600 employees at the time I joined to over 11,000 today, but Jake will still talk to a brand-new rookie on their very first day. It's just the type of person he is. When I had a falling out with Kelly, the number two in my office and my right hand for over 16 years, Jake stepped in and assigned Kristi to be my liaison and help fill that void until we could get back on our feet. He didn't have to do that, but he did. A few years later, when my fiancée got sick and was in the hospital for an extended period of time, we'd talk for hours on the phone. He told me about going through a similar experience with his father and sent me a daily Bible that I started reading every day. That quickly became a part of my morning routine. Those are the type of things Jake did regularly to help people. He reaches out to anyone who is in need of assistance. That leadership style can't help but inspire faith, hope, and confidence in the team. I remember after the Boston Celtics won the NBA championship in 2008, Kevin Garnett said that he would run through a brick wall for his coach Doc Rivers. I think the same thing about Jake. He goes so far above and beyond for his employees that you want to do everything you can for him.

Good leaders inspire others, and for years, Jake wrote a daily email series called #keepplaying where he shared inspirational stories. He then turned that over to the employees, so each day someone different could write their own story about overcoming adversity. I read those stories every morning and find it so incredibly uplifting to learn what some of our employees have been able to accomplish despite the odds. Those stories also reinforce how so many of the principles I've laid out in this book allow people to survive and thrive in their respective storms.

As a leader myself, I have a lot to learn. I know that I can be softer and check in with my employees more often to truly become that person they can trust, but many of the strides I have made in the past couple of years are because of Jake. From him, I've learned about loyalty, and have made it a point to always protect and support my team. If an employee messes something up with a client, we never point the finger. I make sure the responsibility always falls on my shoulders, and I let them know that. And I never let a client disrespect an employee or talk down to them. I'd rather lose the business than have a loan officer crying because some jerk was bullying them.

It doesn't matter whether it's a boss, coach, or mentor, I've learned that the most effective and inspiring leaders are the ones who put themselves on the same level as those they are leading. They don't try to belittle, shame, or scare those beneath them into getting results. Respect is a two-way street, so whether I find myself in the role of leader or I'm turning to someone else for inspiration and guidance, that mutual respect is not only a prerequisite, but it's also the most effective way for everyone involved to achieve their desired results.

Helping Others Helps You

While trying to improve myself, I'm also trying to improve as a coach and leader. I do that through reading, attending summits, and talking to other coaches. I've come a long way and have tried to better gauge when the people I coach need tough love or nurturing. But no matter how much I learn, the one thing that I never waiver on is that I don't let my clients quit. If they've committed to a goal, they can't make excuses. It is my obligation to hold them accountable. That is nonnegotiable, and I can proudly say that I've never worked with someone for an extended period of time who hasn't improved their sales numbers. I get great joy and satisfaction from watching my coaching clients achieve things they didn't think were possible.

When I started working with Mark, his goal was to make more money so he could move closer to the lake. He grew up on a lake and had been driving up there to go sailing with his kids for years, but he was tired of commuting. Being able to make that move became his why, and it's what fueled him. So, we worked on some strategies to help improve his business. He started to see results, and that became the fuel he used to push himself even harder. He did so well that he realized he not only could afford a house near the lake, he could afford a house down the street from the lake. But he didn't stop there.

He kept pushing himself, and today he's in the process of looking for a house *on* the lake. Being able to watch his transformation unfold during our sessions was a really powerful and inspiring experience.

I never could have predicted how much I have gained personally by trying to help others. One of the main reasons why I view coaching as such a fluid process is that the line is often blurred between who's doing the learning and who's doing the coaching. Not only do I enjoy helping others, but I learn as much from being a coach as I do from being coached. Everybody has a book in them, whether they realize it or not. Everybody has a story to tell and wisdom to share.

While coaching recently, I was reminded of a follow-up technique I used to employ years earlier that somehow fell by the wayside when my business evolved. I went back to my team, had them implement that technique, and have already seen the positive results. Clients have told us that they appreciate the communication. And this wasn't a one-time thing. I'm always picking up little tips and valuable information here and there from the people I coach. Whether it's prospecting techniques or upcoming network events, almost every day I pick up on things that I can use myself.

More than anything else, being a coach has helped me learn that while there are many different things that people struggle with, there is most definitely a pattern to how people overcome their obstacles to achieve success. It doesn't matter what their specific goal might be; there is a very clear distinction between what works and what doesn't. A good attitude works—a bad attitude does not. Motivation works—a lack of motivation does not. Individuals with a purpose get further and achieve more success than those who don't know their why. When you break all of this down to its most simple form, those who are willing to put in the work, get out of their comfort zone, try something new, and push themselves will always improve.

EXERCISE

We've talked a lot about how you can get help from others, but what do you have to offer? You may not think of it this way, but chances are that you are in a place that someone else aspires to be. What are you good at? What do you have to offer? Who could you help? If you haven't ever been a coach, try to find a way you can utilize your strengths and your knowledge to give something back to someone else. That could mean coaching a sports team, becoming a Big Brother, or simply taking a younger employee at work under your wing. It doesn't have to be a big commitment but give a coaching a shot. You might be surprised by how much you learn yourself.

The Benefit of Foresight

In 2015, Super Bowl 49 between the New England Patriots and Seattle Seahawks had one of the craziest endings of a Super Bowl ever. Just about everyone who watched that game knows that the Patriots had absolutely no business winning.

The Patriots were down 10 points but clawed their way back and scored a touchdown with 2:02 left in the game to go up 28–24. The Patriots kickoff was a touchback, so the Seahawks could get one play off before the two-minute warning, and quarterback Russell Wilson completed a long pass to Marshawn Lynch that brought them to midfield. With all three timeouts left, the Seahawks started to work the ball down the field, at which point wide receiver Jermaine Kearse made an unbelievable bobbling catch after the ball was tipped multiple times. This set the Seahawks up at the five yard line with 1:06

remaining in the game. As expected, they handed the ball to Marshawn Lynch, who brought it right down to the goal line.

Seattle had three more plays to get it into the endzone, and everyone in the stadium and watching that game on TV expected them to keep handing the ball to Lynch. The way he had been running, it seemed inevitable that he would score, and Seattle would win—but that's not what happened. Instead, Seattle opted to throw the ball. Wilson dropped back and tried to squeeze the ball into the receiver right at the goal line, only for it to be picked off by the Patriots' rookie free agent corner-back Malcolm Butler. The Patriots regained possession and ran out the clock to win the Super Bowl.

For days on end, everyone in the sports community, and even people who knew nothing about football, criticized Seattle for what appeared like such a stupid call to throw the ball on the goal line when they had a running back in Marshawn Lynch who would have surely scored. I wasn't complaining, and nei-ther were any of the Pats fans I knew, but even we had to admit that it was a lucky win. Little did I know what was going on behind the scenes or on the sidelines, and how that Super Bowl victory didn't hinge on poor Seattle play calling in the final seconds as much as on coaching preparation that began many months earlier.

Michael Lombardi was a former Patriots executive who years later wrote a book called *Gridiron Genius: A Master Class in Winning Championships and Building Dynasties in the NFL*. In it, he told a story that I had never heard before about that Super Bowl, and specifically that final play. Lombardi had joined the team at the start of that season and explained how after losing in the playoffs a year earlier, the team set out at the beginning of the season to improve their goal line defense, so they could stop the run. Head Coach Bill Belichick implemented and created what became known as the three-corner defense. Traditional goal line defense is effective against the run because it stacks defenders up against the line, but this alignment was unique because it appeared like a traditional goal line defense but with three cornerbacks that could drop back into pass coverage. What's even more unique about that defense is that after practicing it all preseason, they didn't run it once all season long.

So, when Seattle quarterback Russel Wilson stepped to the line of scrimmage before that final play, it appeared like the Patriots were in goal line defense. That meant if they had handed off the ball to Marshawn Lynch, like everyone thought they would, he most likely wouldn't have scored. The best way to attack that defense was to pass, but with the clock running down, Seattle didn't have time to notice the unique configuration with three corners, and Wilson threw an interception. Most people who watched that unfold thought it was it was poor play calling; what they didn't realize was that it was a carefully laid trap.

When I heard that story, it just reiterated the genius of Bill Belichick as a coach. He practiced a defensive play extensively in preseason for a certain situation that never presented itself all season long, but when it finally did on the last play of the Super Bowl, the most important play of the year, they were ready. He's constantly bashed by the media for being pompous, arrogant, and wanting to make everything about himself, but this story never came out. There are still a lot of hardcore Patriots fans who have never heard this before. Belichick could have easily leaked it if he wanted credit for one of the most memorable Super Bowl victories in history, but he didn't.

Whether we're talking about football, business, or just life, good coaches have foresight and can see things down the road that other people might not be able to. I experienced this personally with my business coach Bill Heart about 12 years ago. At the time, I would send out regular emails to clients and agents with all the information they needed to know. The idea was to keep everyone informed while also stirring up business for myself. For about two years, Bill tried to encourage me to send out videos of myself saying the same thing instead of simply writing it out in an email.

Everyone in the mortgage business at the time was sending out emails like mine. People's inboxes were being flooded with similar messages, so how many of those emails that I regularly sent out were people even reading? Bill could see the future of social media marketing and was trying to guide me in that direction so I could be ahead of the curve, but I fought him on it. Putting myself on video and sending it out felt so incredibly far out of my comfort zone, but he wouldn't let it go. After almost two years of listening to him beat this drum, I brought myself to try it a few times, and I hated it. I didn't think I presented myself well in front of the camera, and I hated watching myself, but then, I noticed something.

The material that I sent out with a video generated more interest and response than the standard email blast. So I finally gave in. I swallowed my pride, stepped out of my comfort zone, and started making more videos. I learned that Bill was right. A lot more people are willing to click on a video than to read an email blast. A lot more people. Over time, the metrics we've kept have proven this to be true. And people weren't just watching them, they were paying attention and responding.

I had fears of how I would look, and what people would say, but none of that came to fruition. What I realized was that nobody cares if you aren't a professional actor. As long as you're real and authentic, people will root for you and want to support you. Nobody wants to see anyone who is genuine fail. That gave me some much-needed confidence that allowed me to step a little further outside of my comfort zone.

Slowly, I converted more of my communication to video. In addition to sending out video updates to clients and agents, I did it with the events we were hosting in the community, with the classes I was offering to the public for first-time homebuyers and with other real estate related topics.

Over time, I learned the benefits went far beyond the actual event I was promoting or information I was trying to convey. I was buying space in people's brains, whether they opened the video or not. If I sent out a video once a week, on a wide variety of topics, people might not open every single one, but they see it every week, and they open the ones about the topics that resonate with them. Either way, I was in their brain, so I was the first person they contacted when they needed the services I provide. That was just one of the many ways that I learned I could expand my business simply by utilizing video instead of an email newsletter. Today, I do everything on video. For two different marathons, I've raised money for charity using video.

Today, utilizing videos is common practice, but Bill saw it coming years in advance. That's what a good coach can do— they can turn you onto trends, techniques, and helpful advice that you might be blind to at the moment. They can bring to your attention what you don't realize you don't know.

* * *

You can only get so far on your own. Alleviate some of the pressure you put on yourself by getting outside help. That can come in the form of a friend, co-worker, employee, or coach. Whether it's delegating tasks that aren't the best use of your time, learning from the experts who have already accomplished what you want to achieve, or having someone looking over your shoulder to hold you accountable and help get you across the finish line, we all need other people in our corner. And never is that more important when you are in the midst of a storm. You are in control of your own destiny, and nobody can do the work for you, but we can all benefit from a helping hand.

CHAPTER 9

From Success to Significance

"Trust yourself. Create the kind of self that you will be happy to live with all your life. Make the most of yourself by fanning the tiny, inner sparks of possibility into flames of achievement."

—Golda Meir

My father never viewed generosity as a value. The way he looked at it was that if he gave something to someone else, he didn't have it anymore. There were so many different ways that I tried to be the opposite of my father growing up, and becoming a generous person was one. It wasn't part of my makeup or how I was wired, but I did try. When I was an altar boy, I used to give some of the money I made from my paper route during the church offering. That was probably the first time I ever gave back.

When I became an adult, giving back was more sporadic. I didn't go out looking for ways to give back, but if there was a good cause that resonated with me, I always tried to give a little more. So, I'd give $5 instead of $1, mainly because I didn't want to be considered cheap. That was how I approached charity for a long time but, in 2006, I set out to make it more of a formal practice.

I had been aware of the Make-A-Wish foundation for years and admired the type of work they did. They are a national organization founded in 1980 that uses charitable donations to provide wishes for kids, between the ages of two and 18, who had been diagnosed with a critical illness. Wishes can be anything from meeting an athlete or celebrity to getting a special gift or going away on a trip.

I had seen that Tom Brady, Rob Gronkowski, David Ortiz, Teddy Bruschi, and a lot of the local Boston athletes were involved with the organization. I also kept seeing Make-A-Wish booths at various business planning events, so that had piqued my interest, but what really sold me on becoming more involved was something I saw when I took a trip down to Disney World with my kids when they were young. We were all in the park together and they were complaining about the heat and wanted to go back to the hotel. The whining was starting to get to me, and right at that moment I saw a group of kids in matching Make-A-Wish tie-dye shirts. Some were in wheelchairs, others were clearly ill, but all of them were smiling ear to ear and having the absolute best time of anyone in the park. That's why they stood out. I was frustrated with my kids and thinking they were spoiled, but at that moment I realized how blessed I was to have a healthy family. I didn't know any of those wish kids or their families, but I knew they had been through a lot and many of them still had such a long road ahead of them. I couldn't imagine the challenges they'd had to face, but despite everything they'd been through, they were having the time of their lives. I thought that if I could help make the road ahead just a little bit easier for kids in that situation, there was no reason for me not to do it, so I did some research into the organization.

The kids come up with their own wishes, and some of them are very clever. One girl in a wheelchair not only had her house made wheelchair accessible but asked for a full-size princess house in the backyard that was also wheelchair accessible. Another boy who was a huge *Lord of the Rings* fan had a hobbit house built into the ground in his backyard. One girl threw a huge mermaid birthday party and invited all of her doctors and nurses from Dana Farber. It turned out that those trips to Disney World were the most popular wishes granted by the foundation, and after seeing what I did in the park that day, I completely understand why. These kids and their families are given the star treatment. They are doted on and first in line for everything.

That year I started making monthly donations, and I haven't missed a month since. The organization keeps the donations private, but often the recipients make themselves known, so we can meet the kids. And from the kids I have met, I can say that they are some of the most unselfish human beings I've ever met. I've also gotten to know their families as well, and they've become involved and helped out with the various fundraisers our company has hosted over the years. It's become quite the network, and it's all about bringing awareness to the organization.

The cause hit close to home back in 2012 when my cousin, who was 17 and suffering from muscular dystrophy, became a wish recipient. I was able to convince my aunt to enroll before he turned 18 and would no longer be eligible. Muscular dystrophy is such a horrible disease. My cousin had lost the use of his limbs, so what he wished for was a specially designed Apple computer that allowed him to communicate. Unfortunately, he has since passed away, but I witnessed how much that computer helped him, and I believe, without a doubt, that it was able to prolong his life and make things just a little bit easier for him and his family.

In school, I was taught about tithing, which is giving 10 percent of your income to the church, but today, I like to think of tithing as giving back to where you get your spiritual nutrition from. And that's what Make-A-Wish does for me. Seeing the impact those wishes can have on those kids and their families is where I get a big part of my spiritual nutrition from. I can't overstate the importance of giving back, but a lot of people are struggling to stay above water themselves and find it hard to part with any portion of what they earn, especially when times are tough. I understand how difficult this can be, but I can't stress the importance of finding a way to make it work. It doesn't have to be money, but if you look closely enough, you might also be surprised to find that the sacrifice is not nearly the burden it might initially seem.

In 2008, one year after I committed to giving money to Make-A-Wish, I was having a bad year. My whole business was in the red. My accounting team told me that I had to cut expenses, and the first thing they wanted me to eliminate were the donations. I thought about it, and then told them, "We're going to cut everything but that." I had made a commitment and I was serious about keeping it. That was important to me.

That forced me to look closely at where we were spending money. Instead of buying supplies at W. B. Mason or Staples, we shopped at BJ's and saved a couple hundred bucks. The closer I looked, the more I found ways to save. It opened my eyes to waste and ways that my business could run more smoothly. Not only did I find enough money to cover the donation, but with the added savings, I actually came out ahead. The ancillary benefit was that it also made me incredibly motivated. I had made a commitment, and I didn't want to flake, so I went into supersales mode that further accelerated my business. Just by making sure I could maintain that commitment, I trimmed the fat and amped up my production. Quite the silver lining.

If you aren't sure that you have the money to give back, take a look at your spending habits. Go over your bank account. Examine your credit card statements. Look closely at where you're spending money. Are you spending $10 a day at Starbucks? Are you going out too many nights? I guarantee you that if you look hard enough, you will find a way to give back that 10 percent, so that you won't even miss it. I promise you that if you're able to make a difference and impact the world in a way that you haven't before, you will not only feel better about yourself, but it will come back around to benefit you tenfold.

I've been discussing this in terms of money, but don't forget that donating money isn't the only way you can give back. You can donate your time and get involved in the community. If you're stuck and can't think of ideas, start with where you get your spiritual nutrition from. Remember that you can't keep a negative and positive thought in your mind at the same time. Try volunteering for a cause close to your heart, and see how many negative thoughts enter your mind. When you truly feel that you're making a difference and contributing to something bigger than yourself, it's very difficult to focus on negatives. That alone is extremely powerful.

I don't think it's a coincidence that every year that I increased my donation, my income from that year also increased. The more generous I became, the more success I experienced. This is really difficult to explain to some people, and I understand their skepticism. Call it the law of attraction, the abundance mentality, or the natural law of gratitude, but what you give finds its way back to you. Tithing, giving, generosity, volunteering, and contribution have opened me up to receiving more than anything else in this world. It's positive karma, and that can make me feel good no matter how awful everything else is—but there is a catch.

Any giving has to be unconditional. Donations are often made for positioning, influence, and appearances. There are tangible benefits that come from giving back, but that's not what I'm talking about. You can't just give in order to get back or give begrudgingly. It has to be genuine, or don't bother at all. However, I will say from experience that when you're doing something for others, and genuinely put in the effort to make a difference, it's difficult to be selfish.

I like to think that the whole philosophy behind giving back has bled over into my day-to-day life to make me a better person. Today, I make sure to do the little things. When I ask someone how they're doing, I try to really mean it, and not just make it a formality. How often do you walk by someone and ask, "How you doing" while barely making eye contact? You don't mean it, and they could be having the absolute worst day and still answer "Fine." I've made it a point to be better at not only listening but hearing and understanding. I check in with people when they're down and try to make them feel important. All of these things were very difficult for me at first, and didn't even occur to me for a while, but the more I practiced and made an effort, the more natural they become, and the more I reaped the spiritual benefits.

EXERCISE

What is one way that you can start giving back? It doesn't have to be money, but it certainly can be. There are a lot of national and local causes that are worth donating to. You could volunteer your time and try to make a difference that way. Start with what interests you and what opportunities might be available in your community. Talk with your friends or co-workers to see what opportunities they know that you might not be aware of. The only prerequisite is that it has to be genuine. You can't do it in the hope that you will get something back in return.

It's Never Too Early to Consider Your Legacy

In 1999, my father was in the process of being medically retired from the fire department for a back injury when the Worcester Warehouse Fire occurred. Two homeless people who were squatting in the 93-year-old abandoned building knocked over a candle and set the massive six-story warehouse on fire. Units from all over the area were called in, but it only got worse, and six firefighters were still trapped inside when the building collapsed. The rescue effort was all over the news, and it went on for eight days, but my father never joined. When I asked him why, he told me, "If I go down to help, there is a good chance that they think I can still do the job, so I won't get medically retired and won't get paid."

I couldn't believe what I was hearing. "Do you know how pathetic that sounds? The guys you work with, your brothers, are buried under the rubble, and you aren't going to go look for them because you think you might lose money?"

He didn't only rub me the wrong way, most of the people he worked with felt the same way. When you retire, the other firefighters usually throw you a huge party and make a big deal out of retirement. But my dad? Nothing. And he was a captain, and nobody gave a damn when he retired. He was just that much of an asshole.

After that, we got into a huge fight and I kept my distance from my father, but I never shut him completely out of my life. More than anything, I tolerated him. Today, we don't talk much. He lives about five miles down the road from me, so I can't completely ignore him. I see him at my nieces and nephews' birthday parties and some other family events. When I had kids and they started to get older, he made an attempt to be a part of their lives. I wasn't going to ever prevent that from happening.

For a while, I tried to make things right. I pushed him to change in the hope that he would want to leave some kind of legacy behind. "What's it going to say on your tombstone when you die? Is it just going to be your name and the days you were born and died? What impact will you have made?" I think that's a pretty powerful question, because who wants to leave nothing behind? He didn't have a good answer, and that didn't seem to bother him at all. It clearly wasn't a priority, but I'd always tell him that it wasn't too late to turn things around. In 2010, I tried to get him a job as a limo driver, but he wouldn't do it. It was the same excuses all of the time. "If I ever get caught with another job, I could lose my pension." I was trying to get him to just go out there and live life, but he had this rigid and close-minded way of thinking that felt so pathetic to me.

I'd get worked up about it and tell this to my therapist at the time, and she finally said, "Bill, you can't change someone else if they don't want to change. You've expressed your desire to help, but if he doesn't want to change, he's never going to."

Hearing that, it felt like a burden was lifted. It completely changed the way I interacted with him. Now I wish him the best and throw positive vibes out there, but that's all I can do at this point. I also know that it's never too late. He can still change, and I hope he does. The fact that my father might not leave behind any legacy has made it that much more of a priority for me to have a legacy of my own, but over the years, what that legacy is and even the definition of the word has evolved.

For the longest time, I associated success with achievement—be it physical or professional. That came with accomplishment and financial success, so when I first became interested in the world of self-development, most of my goals were sales and numbers related. There was a point where I assumed success led to happiness, and that if I just had the financial security that I hadn't had in my life up to that point, I would finally be set. Then I hit those sales and financial goals. My why began to evolve and with it my definition of legacy. When you become successful, you learn that success doesn't always lead to fulfillment. Think about all of the so-called successful people living lives others envy who wind up depressed and sometimes kill themselves. I've learned that the missing link that prevents many successful people from achieving fulfillment is significance, and for me, that speaks directly to legacy.

What started for me as a pursuit of success has evolved into a pursuit of fulfillment and significance. It's about being able to impact not just my own family, but to make a difference for as many other families as possible. That to me is another, all-encompassing form of success. You do that by leading a good life, setting an example, and making the world a better place. I've learned the way to do that is by leading, volunteering and contributing. Today, that is where I find significance. And it's a daily pursuit. That's what I hope people will say about me when I'm six feet under. I hope that I encourage my kids, and later my grandkids, to do the same through the positive example I set.

I hope that one day they make a difference in the world, and don't just aimlessly drift through life.

My grandfather was one of my best friends growing up. He protected me from my dad, and he rooted for me in ways that my father never would. He took an interest in what I did and made me want to be better. It broke my heart when he was diagnosed with esophageal cancer, and we found that he didn't have long to live. After my freshman football season, I told him that I was going to be a starter my sophomore year. That made me want to make that dream a reality, and I did. Even though he was in poor health, he would come out to those games to watch me play. When I was on the sidelines, I could hear him coughing up in the stands, and that motivated me to play even harder. My grandfather passed away soon after that, and his legacy is solidified in my mind as someone who was there. Sometimes, that's all it takes. It's showing up to be the best parent, grandparent, or friend you can be. It's giving yourself, your time, being kind, and helping others. That's often overlooked, but it's those actions that can leave the most lasting impact.

Don't wait until you experience a certain level of success to begin thinking about legacy. Unfortunately, that's what too many people do. They say, "But I can't start thinking about legacy until I get my life together." No! It doesn't matter if you don't yet have your life together. If you're aimless, drifting, or in debt, that's the perfect time to begin thinking about legacy. What most people don't realize until it's too late is that legacy is directly connected to your why—they fuel each other.

Take Time to Enjoy the Journey
You shouldn't just celebrate the little milestones and small wins along the way; you should make sure that you take the time to

celebrate yourself and everything you've done to get there. In other words, take the time to enjoy the journey.

I've always been a guy with a powerful motor. My core genius is grit and determination, so when it comes to pushing my limits, that might be less difficult for me than others. But I became so focused on the process and working toward my goals that whenever I achieved something, I never took the time to celebrate the accomplishment or reward myself. I had blinders on. Maybe I made some time for a few high fives and a couple of beers, but I quickly turned my attention to the next thing. As soon as I earned my black belt, I turned my attention to the marathon, then the Ironman, and when that was complete, I focused on being a top producer in my company and having a career year. I not only didn't celebrate my accomplishments, but a part of me blatantly avoided them, because I didn't want to be soft, let up, or pull any focus from the next goal I was trying to accomplish. It didn't matter how much I accomplished or how far ahead I got; this became a pattern in everything I did.

Whenever I signed a client or made a big deal, instead of reveling in it, I worried about where the next one was going to come from. Would be able to pay my bills down the road? During a time when I should have been happy, I'd lose sleep at night worrying about things that were out of my control.

I may have thought I was pushing myself to be better, but what I was really doing was focusing on what I didn't have when I needed to focus on the opposite. If I had taken the time to enjoy those accomplishments and celebrate with the people who I care about, it could have been less stressful for me, my friends, and my family.

You need to stop and smell the roses. Enjoy the sunsets and sunrises. Today, I look for ways to incorporate that into the process in order to make it more enjoyable and rewarding.

Whenever I run on the beach, I make sure to look out over the ocean and remember what it is that I enjoy so much about what I'm doing, instead of hurrying up and trying to get something done by a certain time, so I can rush on to the next thing. Even when it comes to actual competition, there is so much beauty out there, so whenever I'm running or participating in an event outdoors, I've learned how to tap into that and use it as fuel to lift me up. I take the time to enjoy the crowd and let them carry me when possible. No matter what I'm doing, I become more aware of my surroundings and allow myself to think: *This is freaking awesome!*

My attitude at work has changed as well. I've been in the mortgage business for 23 years and have closed over a billion dollars in volume, but I still get excited about every single application I take. And I take about 12 a week, which is over 600 a year. Yes, I still get excited about every single one of them. And guess what? That creates momentum, so I actually get even more. Ever since I learned how to let go and celebrate, every single year has been better than the year before. That attitude has calmed me down more than anything else.

I've even taken this a step further and have learned to enjoy watching others succeed as well. I've applied this to my business, so whenever the team gets a positive review, we make sure to celebrate it as a team. When an individual does something noteworthy or goes above and beyond, we acknowledge them and make sure they're rewarded.

Whether you celebrate a victory or worry if it's going to be your last, that energy creates momentum. Believe it or not, negative welcomes negative, and positive welcomes positive. I can say, without a doubt, that once I learned to loosen up, stop worrying, and celebrate my victories, no matter how small, I achieved even more personal and professional success.

EXERCISE

Go back to that exercise where you audited your day and look at it from a different perspective. This time around, don't pay as much attention to what you're doing as to what you might *not* be doing. Look at your routine and ask yourself what you aren't seeing, savoring, or appreciating. Maybe you hate your commute to work every day, but don't take the time to consider the beautiful scenery you pass through. Instead of complaining and making yourself feel miserable for being stuck in the car, enjoy the beauty that is right outside your window. That may not apply to you, but I promise you that there is something you do on a regular basis that you can look at from a different perspective and learn to enjoy.

The Power of Reading Your Own Obituary

Alfred Nobel was a Swedish scientist, businessman, and philanthropist known for establishing the Nobel Prize, but not many people know about the origin of the award.

Alfred followed in the footsteps of his father, who was an engineer and owner of weapon and mine factories. Alfred filed for his first of 355 patents at the age of 24, and went on to develop nitroglycerine detonators, blasting caps, and his most famous invention, gunpowder, in 1867. Though very successful, he was developing quite a reputation as a war monger and a merchant of death. But this never impacted him until he found himself in the unique position of reading his own obituary.

In 1888, Alfred's brother Ludvig died of a heart attack while in France. Some of the local newspapers thought that it was Alfred who died, so that's whose obituary they wrote and printed. The newspapers claimed, "the merchant of death is dead," and explained how he got rich by creating new ways to kill people faster, and how his only contribution to the world was death and destruction. Alfred Nobel had the rare experience of reading about what people "really" thought of him. That was enough to get him to change his ways and chart a different course, though he told very few people, even leaving his family in the dark.

In 1895, at the age of 62, Alfred laid out in his will his plans to devote the majority of his fortune, which translates to roughly $265 million in today's dollars, to what has become known as the Nobel Prize. It began as a series of prizes for people who made discoveries that benefited mankind in five key areas: physics, chemistry, medicine, literature, and spreading peace. Family members were furious that they wouldn't inherit most of his wealth. After Alfred died of a stroke in his home of Sanremo, Italy, family bickering ensued for a few years before the foundation was finally established and the awards handed out for the first time in 1901. The program itself has evolved and expanded, but the awards have been handed out every year since on December 10, the anniversary of Alfred Nobel's death. Had any of that happened, and would there be a Nobel Prize, if Alfred hadn't read that obituary? It's impossible to say, but there is no denying its impact.

When I first heard that story, I couldn't help but start thinking about how people will remember me, because there can be a big difference between how I want to be remembered and how I will be remembered, but today I do my best to bridge that gap, so they become one and the same. What will people say about you and what will you leave behind?

EXERCISE

Take out a pen and paper and write down what you believe people will say about you at your eulogy. There is a distinction between what you want people to say about you and what people actually will say about you. Take note of that difference, because that's a very good indication of what you need to work on in this area.

Don't get so caught up in a self-help journey that you forget about the world around you and the people in your life. True success is about so much more than money and career accomplishments. You don't want your eulogy to be a reading of your resume. You want it to be about the impact you had on the world. You want it to be about the love you gave and how you made a difference in the lives of those around you for the better. That doesn't happen all at once. That happens over time through the little things you do every day and being able to give back as much as you take. If you learn how to make that a habit, you can't help but become significant in the long run.

EPILOGUE
There Will Always Be Another Storm

I started training to run my fifth Boston Marathon in the summer of 2021. It had been pushed from the usual April date to October because of COVID. I also had my eye on the future. My daughter was turning 18 in October, and she wanted to go skydiving, so we planned on doing that together. I signed up for another Ironman later in 2021 as well, and intended to get my second-degree black belt before the end of the year. I was striving for another record year at work, along with getting more into professional coaching. It was a great plan, but all of that changed on Tuesday, August 10, 2021.

Just like every other day, it was dark out when I woke up at 5:00 a.m. I was running late, so I was trying to play catch-up. On my way downstairs to make my coffee and get ready for my run, I missed the last two stairs. I had my phone and a

191

glass of water in my hand, and both went flying. I managed to catch myself before falling but jammed my leg into the floor and dropped to the ground. I looked down and saw a bulge in my quad, and felt the most pain I had ever experienced before in my life. I'm not exaggerating. I thought I had broken my leg, and that the bone was sticking out. Upon further, hesitant, examination, it was squishy to the touch, so it wasn't a broken bone. I tried to get up a few times, but that wasn't happening. I knew that I had done some serious damage.

I was alone in the house and had to crawl across the floor to get to the phone so I could call my ex-wife, Stephanie, for help. She arrived shortly after and had to help me into the car. I felt white-hot blinding pain. I was beyond crying, and surprised that I didn't pass out. I had torn my bicep on two different occasions, and that was a walk in the park compared to what I was experiencing.

When we arrived at the hospital, the doctor gave me an X-ray, but didn't bother doing an MRI because he could tell what happened. "You ruptured the tendon in your quad. It's not attached to the bone anymore, so you need surgery."

By that point, my only surprise was that it wasn't any worse. We reached out to the head of orthopedics who had performed one of my bicep surgeries years earlier, and he was available to do it the next day. They loaded me up on pain-killers and sent me home that night. I set myself up on the recliner, and in a fog, started Googling my injury. I thought it said recovery time was six to eight weeks. The marathon was in two months, so I immediately started texting people, saying that I would still be able to do it. When I arrived for surgery in the morning, I asked the doctor if he thought it was possible, and he looked at me like I was crazy. It turns out that recovery time was not six to eight weeks, but six to eight months. "You're not running any marathon," he told me with a straight face.

Suddenly, the reality of my situation sank in. I sat with that feeling and tried to process my options. I could easily set myself up on the recliner for the next couple of months, and have my family make my meals, while I focused on work and physical therapy so that I could heal. Nobody would blame me for that, and I wouldn't fault anyone in my situation for taking it easy, but I knew myself. I knew that would have made me so freaking depressed. I knew that I needed to keep my mind occupied and take massive action.

I also thought about this book, and the message I had been preaching in these pages. I realized that I needed to set an example, follow through on what I've been saying, and put my money where my mouth is, or else I would be a fraud. There are too many of those people out there and I didn't want to be another one. This was another storm, and if I truly believed anything I had written in these pages, I would follow through and practice what I preach, and live what I was talking about. This was the perfect opportunity for me to test the process.

I returned home after surgery with a new plan and got back on the computer to see if I would be able to complete the marathon on crutches. There were people who had done it before, but they changed protocol after the 2013 bombing, so they wouldn't allow anyone on the course with crutches. I had to limp it, or I couldn't do it at all. That was deflating, but then I learned that because of COVID, you could sign up to complete the 2021 marathon virtually. That meant that I could do it at a different location, and on my own time, which wouldn't preclude using crutches. That looked like a possible option.

I had planned to run for Make-A-Wish again, so the day after my surgery, I emailed them to see if this was something they could help arrange. The coordinator offered her apologies, but I don't think she took me seriously because she mentioned liability issues and said she would formally withdraw me from the race. No! Within seconds of seeing that email, I replied back, begging her not to withdraw me from the race. Eventually, she told me that they would keep my spot open. I reached out to my Make-A-Wish rep Peg, whom I had been working closely with for over 14 years, and she agreed to help me make the arrangements and find a location to complete the marathon virtually.

That fired me up! With a recovery time of six to eight months, I knew that I needed something to work toward that would occupy my mind and take my attention off everything else I was dealing with. I didn't want anyone taking that away from me. However, I quickly realized that I was in uncharted territory, and had no idea how or if I was going to be able to pull something like this off.

Then I thought about the Make-A-Wish kids who I'd be running for, and how my situation could help raise funds and bring awareness to the cause. *What's nine hours of discomfort compared to what some of those kids have to go through?* When you get to meet them and get to know their families, you learn about real sacrifice. Some of them have to commute 60 miles each way, just to get to the hospital for treatment. Some are in a fight for their lives; others have to go through treatment for years. If the pain some of these kids were forced to endure wasn't enough, the personal and financial strain that this puts on their families is devastating. Add COVID to the mix and the struggles multiply, but those kids and their families don't have a choice in the matter. All that happened to me was a minor setback. It sucked, and it was an obstacle, but I would survive and recover. Once I started thinking like that, I knew there was no way that I wouldn't do it. My why was in place, and it couldn't have been stronger.

There were still some problems to resolve. We didn't have a location yet, and I wasn't really sure how I was going to pull any of this off. But I knew from experience that when the why is strong enough, the how doesn't matter. I had 60 days before Marathon Monday on Columbus Day. I immediately created a checklist. Before I dove into preparation and training, the first thing I had to do was declare my goals. So, I changed my Facebook page from "running for wishes" to "crutching for wishes." I let everyone know what I was going to do and began to raise money. Many of the families of the kids we got to know reached out and donated, but not before some of the moms gave me a hard time for not taking the time to get better. I had just created built-in accountability, so I wouldn't be able to back out now.

The next step was to research and learn everything possible about what I was trying to do, but there was one big problem—there isn't much of anything written about how to complete a marathon on crutches. A few people had done it, many of whom were amputees, but there wasn't any Google Image training program that I could download this time around. I was all on my own.

It would all come down to preparation. I immediately dove into physical therapy to begin rehabbing my leg. I set aside time to get on regular chiropractic and massage regiments. My sister Kelly was an acupuncturist, and she came to the house to work with me. I knew that all of this would speed up my recovery, as would learning about the necessary nutrition and supplements. Then I got on the crutches and reality came crashing down around me. My underarms chafed, my shoulders killed, my hip hurt because it was out of alignment, and both my legs were cramping—even my good leg hurt. It was uncomfortable and painful, but worst of all, I was slow—it took me an hour and a half to complete only one mile. I did the math and realized at that rate it would take me over a day to finish the marathon. *This is going to suck!*

This injury was legit, and I had greatly underestimated the goal I had set out to achieve. I was going to need help, because there was no way I could do this on my own. So, I went to the experts—my doctors, physical therapists, nutritionist, massage therapist, and all of my different coaches—and said, "I need your help." I told them, "This is what I'm going to do. I'm pretty sure it's going to go against everything you recommend, but I am committed, and I need you to teach me how to do this right and prepare."

And guess what? Every single one of them helped. They not only showed me exactly what I needed to do, but they worked harder with me than they did anyone else because I asked for help. They knew I wanted to learn, and I was coachable, so they did everything they could to get me ready. Whether it was learning extra PT drills that I could do at home, or Kelly agreeing to come to my house to perform acupuncture, everyone played a role, and I wouldn't have been able to come close to accomplishing what I set out to achieve without them.

I picked up some techniques that allowed me to go a little faster, while putting less stress on my leg and shoulders. I was still a very far cry away from being able to crutch for 26.2 miles, but I wasn't even thinking of that, because I knew that if the why was strong enough, the how would take care of itself. And there is no better proof of that then what happened next.

Peg, my rep from Make-A-Wish, got on the phone and started making calls to see what they could arrange, and unbeknownst to me, they reached out to Tom McNamara at my alma mater, Worcester State, to inquire if it would be possible for someone to use their track to complete the marathon virtually. First, he said he'll see what he could do, but then she told him I was an alum, and when he found out who, he said, "Oh, Bill Murphy? Anything he needs!"

I thought that was so cool. I know Tom from some charity work in the past, but more from my contribution to the school over the years. Because I always regretted not playing college football, I'd been giving two scholarships to the school since 2006 for Worcester State students who attended my high school. They just have to be commuters enrolled in an extracurricular activity—anything except organized sports, because that would be a violation of NCAA rules. In 2007, I was given a distinguished alumni award for charitable donations. That same year, I started an internship program, hiring two interns from Worcester State to work for me. I still do that today, and we end up hiring a lot of those students full time after they graduate. And every so often, I'll speak to a few of the business classes. It was just another reminder of how what you give comes back to you tenfold, often in ways you could have never anticipated.

Things were falling into place, and I made sure to celebrate those victories because I knew how important it was to remain positive. I firmly believe that anger, hostility, blame, and constant complaining can bring you down and, in some cases, cripple you. People can literally make themselves sick with their negative thoughts. If that's true, the opposite is true as well, and you can literally make yourself feel better with positive thoughts. For me, it goes back to the runner's high and those feelings of elation and euphoria that come from releasing endorphins.

More than ever, I had a reason to slip into a negative mindset, but as soon as I caught myself reminiscing about the way things used to be with my wife, placing blame, or feeling sorry for myself after getting hurt, I immediately stopped and remind myself of what I was thankful for. I thought of my kids, and my staff. When your thoughts go negative, you want to change your mindset and focus on the blessings as quickly as possible. Don't indulge or allow your brain to go down that avenue, because those negative emotions will raise your stress levels and the cortisol in your body. Keep it positive, and you can have the opposite effect.

I started using those feelings of belief, faith, hope, and certainty as healing energy. I literally started breathing positive energy into my leg, and I'm not exaggerating when I say that it made a difference. Yes, I made a lot of sacrifices and set aside the time to train. I made sure my nutrition was on point, and I bought all of the equipment I could to do the PT exercises at home. Add visualization and the positive story I kept telling myself again and again and again whenever a shred of doubt ever entered my mind, and it worked. My doctors and physical therapists couldn't believe the progress I was making. After five weeks of physical therapy, they told me it looked like I had been rehabbing for 10 weeks. They hadn't seen an injury like mine heal so fast before. I started putting weight on my leg two weeks earlier than expected, and I know it had everything to do with my mindset.

I was starting to see other benefits as well, benefits that I could have never anticipated. I set out trying to achieve this goal as a way to show perseverance, dedication, resilience, and commitment as an example for my children that I would do whatever it took. From the very beginning, they were with me. They thought it was cool. My mother also made herself available to help me every way she possibly could. This was just another example of how my mother would always be there, no matter what. I make sure to never forget it, and she remains an example for me when it comes to how I parent my own children.

It may not seem like it in the moment, but every storm has a silver lining, and not long after I suffered this injury, I discovered the silver lining of this situation when my kids came to stay with me. Before I got hurt, I couldn't have paid them to stay with me, but we started spending more time together and it was awesome. When I was coming down the stairs one morning, my youngest asked me if I needed help. All of my kids started working together to make me food and change my sheets. I didn't even know my kids could do some of these things. They had my back, and that has brought all of us closer together.

I noticed that I was making great personal strides as well. My spirituality had never been stronger, and I was more vigilant with journaling and meditation, so those habits became more ingrained in my life. Becoming more aware of my thoughts has been grounding and helped me overcome adversity.

When something unexpected, negative, or downright catastrophic happens, you have to get in the habit of looking for the blessing. This is so hard to do, because your brain is going to want to find an excuse instead, and there will be some good ones, so if you listen closely, you can convince yourself to quit or even not start at all. But once you start looking for those silver linings and hidden blessings, you can't help but find them. The more I thought about it, the more grateful I became that it was my left leg that I hurt. If I had hurt my right leg, I wouldn't have been able to drive and that would have completely changed the nature of my recovery. I reached a point where I became legitimately grateful for that. The silver linings are there. You just have to be open and receptive, but that's never going to happen if you don't feel the feelings and go through the grieving process.

Meanwhile, I was getting stronger, and I was getting faster. My strategy was to increase my mileage every single week, but time was not on my side. I couldn't train for this like I could if I were running the marathon. I needed to build up my endurance and get used to spending extended periods of time on the crutches. That meant increasing my mileage at a time when I would normally be tapering off.

Through it all, I continued to work out five or six days a week. I kept up my cardio by using the Arc Trainer. It wasn't nearly as intense, but I was still able to work my upper body. I was also going to PT twice a week and did absolutely everything I possibly could to accelerate the healing process. What began as being able to only do one or two laps around the quarter-mile track evolved into two miles. That became five, and then seven. Every day, I was able to distribute more and more weight to my bad leg. Pretty soon, I was walking short distances at home without crutches at all. Because I hadn't been able to put weight on my leg for so long, it had atrophied significantly, and there was no muscle at all on my thigh. It was actually kind of depressing to look at. Once I was able to keep both feet on the ground, and briskly walk around the track with the aid of the crutches, I was finally able to regain some strength, but there are always new obstacles and challenges to overcome, many of which I had never encountered before, or even expected to encounter.

First it was the chafing that set me back. The burning under my armpits was unbearable at times, so I spoke with my physical therapists to learn what I could do, and then ordered the best crutches on the market. They were ergonomically designed to help prevent that very issue. These things were the Cadillac of crutches, and that finally gave me some much-needed relief, so I could get back at it. That helped the chafing, but other little problems kept popping up that I hadn't anticipated.

When I started hitting 10 miles, my knees were bothering me—not just my injured left knee, but also my right because I was overcompensating. That meant I had to go out and get these new compression knee braces that could alleviate the tension.

As my training increased, and I started going longer and longer distances, my hands were getting numb from the crutches, so I found myself stopping to shake them out quite a bit. That meant another readjustment. I had to loosen my grip on the crutches. During the process, I learned to lengthen my stride and getting the crutches far enough out in front of me, so I didn't have to put too much weight on my bad leg.

These were all things that I had never thought of before. It was like figuring out a new form of calisthenics that my body wasn't used to, but the more I worked and the more time I spent on the crutches, the more I saw results. I was able to increase both my distance and my time. I told myself that all I had to do was get 1 percent better every day, and by the time the marathon rolled around I would be ready. Eventually I got up to 13 miles, and I was feeling less and less uncomfortable. The following week, I pushed myself to get 17 before I maxed out a week before the marathon with 19. That gave me a week to rest. I'd do a couple miles here and there just to stay loose, but nothing crazy.

I became addicted to the process and making progress. Whenever I was able to improve my time, I celebrated that minor victory, instead of rushing to the next milestone. I even found ways to play games with myself to make it easier. The track where I worked out was right near a children's soccer practice field. For a while, it was good entertainment while I did endless laps around the track for hours on end. Each game would go an hour, and there were three of them, so that was three hours' worth of distractions. I was always dodging the occasional dogs and kids running across the track, but I was well entertained. Then, I thought of it a different way and started to get paranoid because I didn't want parents to see some me and think that I was some kind of whack-job predator. Finally, that got the best of me, and I decided to change up tracks.

In the meantime, word was getting out and I was attracting attention—the good kind of attention. I wasn't looking to promote myself. I didn't want the publicity; I wanted to promote Make-A-Wish to raise more money, so that's what I had been doing on Facebook. A couple of weeks before the race, Tom Brady was scheduled to make his return to Foxboro to play the New England Patriots for the first time since he became a member of the Tampa Bay Buccaneers. It was a once-in-a-lifetime game at Gillette Stadium, and a very hot ticket, so I decided to raffle off a pair of tickets on my Facebook page to the highest bidder, with all the proceeds going to Make-A-Wish. One of the guys bidding was named Dennis Murphy, and everyone jokingly accused me of rigging the raffle, but I had no idea who he was. It turned out that he won the raffle and reached out to me and said he would have kept bidding no matter how high the tickets got because his daughter was a Make-A-Wish recipient five years earlier, and the cause was important to him.

Throughout the entire process, I kept making videos, and they were getting thousands more views than any other videos I had made for previous races. People were identifying with what I was doing. They reached out to me, and every day I was getting messages from people who I didn't even know telling me how what I was doing motivated them to overcome their own ailments. That was really cool to hear. And they weren't just reaching out to me. Worcester State and Make-A-Wish were getting interview requests. And the donations were coming in from all over, and they continued to right up until the race. That had been the goal the entire time. That was the why. I was able to raise over $20,000 for Make-A-Wish. Ironically, I wouldn't have nearly been able to raise that much money had I not gotten hurt. Another silver lining.

A few days before the race, my new goal was to finish in eight hours. I was with my buddies on Cape Cod, and I tried to get them to take bets on whether I'd be able to hit that goal with all proceeds going to Make-A-Wish, but I didn't have any takers. They saw how much I had improved, and didn't want to bet against me, but they all agreed to donate anyway, which I thought was cool of them.

Marathon Monday was on Columbus Day, Monday, October 11, so together with Make-A-Wish and Worcester State, we arranged for me to do it the day before on Sunday, which was the day that worked best for everyone involved. My idea was to start at 4:00 a.m. I figured that's when most people are sleeping, so by the time they got up, I'd be almost done.

I was up at about 2:15 a.m. that morning. I prepped my bag with all my energy bars, salts, drinks, and everything else I needed. A friend gave me a ride to the track. My family, a few other friends, representatives from Make-A-Wish, and even a few wish kids were there for support. Still, I hated the waiting around. At 3:58 a.m., I had enough and just started going. Keep in mind this was Sunday morning on a college campus, so for the first hour I managed to stay entertained by a few of the kids making the walk of shame back to their dorm rooms before the sun came up.

I got off to a fast start and was flying in the beginning. I knew that I would have to slow down if I got fatigued, but my energy and adrenaline weren't wavering, so I kept it up. I had forgotten the Vaseline to help with the chafing under my armpits, so by mile nine I was in rough shape, but I had no choice but to keep going. I had to block it out of my mind. I did get hungry, but I could do something about that. The only time I stopped was to grab a banana, or take a drink of water, but I kept moving.

Eventually my pace started to taper off as the race progressed. By the time I hit mile 20, I was going significantly slower, but with only two miles to go, something interesting and completely unexpected happened. A 13-year-old girl started to walk fast and keep up alongside me. Her name was Bethany, and she was one of the wish kids who was there watching. Immediately, she started talking. "I think it's so cool that you're doing this!"

I was shocked at first. "I think it's so cool you're here," I told her.

She went on to talk about how she had overcome pancreatitis, and how the trip to Disney that Make-A-Wish had provided helped her recovery and overall health so much that she went on to become an ambassador. She told me that what she remembers most were the smiles she saw on her parents' faces. I think people dismiss that, but these kids are so used to seeing their parents crying and feeling overwhelmed. And even though they might not be completely pain-free during a week-long trip to Disney, it's just a little bit of relief, and those memories also have tremendous healing power that can propel them through the next round of chemo, or the next surgery. It gives them strength.

Bethany was such an enthusiastic ball of energy that I couldn't help but pick up my pace. When I later went back and looked at the app that charted the race for me, those last two miles were faster than the first two, and it was all because of the energy that I received from her. It was contagious. She was the one who coached me and carried me to the finish line. And after 105 trips around the track, I finished the virtual Boston Marathon in six hours and 17 minutes.

Not only did I blow away my own goal, but I came really close to breaking a world record for completing a marathon on crutches. It was around the 20-mile mark that someone told me I was close to the record, and it was fun to chase, but I also knew that most of the people competing for those records were amputees, so it wasn't exactly an evening playing field. That's why when Make-A-Wish tried to reach out to Guinness, I was like, "No! Guys, really? That's not important to me." I wasn't about to broadcast that because I knew that I'd look like a jerk.

I made sure to enjoy the accomplishment, but even that happened in unexpected ways. A few days later, I was at a high school football game with my buddy watching his son play, and was wobbling down the bleachers, when someone called out, "Hey, that guy just ran a marathon on crutches!" Things like that have happened a few times, and I've had other people who I've never met reach out to me online, which is pretty wild. One of the most pleasant and touching surprises occurred shortly after the marathon, when I read my daughter's college essay about how what I had done inspired her to follow her dreams and reinforced the idea that she could accomplish anything she put her mind to. I couldn't have been prouder after reading that, and it makes me feel like I had done my job as a parent. When I was lying on the floor after suffering that injury, I could never have expected so many positive things could materialize from something that seemed so unfortunate at the time.

Those 60 days leading up to the marathon were a whirlwind. I had been laser focused on a goal and put everything into achieving it, but with the race over and my goal accomplished, I couldn't help but wonder what was going to happen next. Training for the marathon had occupied my mind. If I didn't have that, I could have easily gotten lost. Now, I wouldn't need the crutches anymore, so I could do a little bit more modified exercise. I'd be able to start jogging in a few weeks, but would that be enough? I wish that I could say that I have evolved over the years, learned to take my own advice, and was able to fill that void elsewhere, but I was restless.

My first thought went to earning my second-degree black belt. That had been delayed because of COVID, and before I got hurt, I had planned to start training three days after the marathon with a bootcamp. If I had run the marathon on crutches, maybe there was an outside chance I could do that, too. I went to my doctor, and he did a couple tests, but told me there was absolutely no way that I could do what was required to earn my black belt. I couldn't jump, kick, or grapple on the ground. Krav Maga is a combat sport and with one wrong move, I could do permanent damage. I convinced him to write me a note to participate in some drills, but he told me that I should wait another two months at the earliest before doing anything serious. I started going again, but it just wasn't the same. I had to sit out some drills, and it became clear very early on that no matter what my mind was telling me, I would not be able to compete with everyone physically. Unlike the marathon, I wouldn't be able to do it smart and safe. There was really no way around that, so I had to resign myself to postponing another goal.

I have come to terms with the fact that I need to heal. I'm taking the time to sit with the situation and see what comes to me instead of racing off to the next thing. My daughter wants to do a triathlon, so I know that in time I can help her with that. Pretty soon, I can start swimming laps at the Y and biking on the Peloton. I have to wait a few months before I can start running again, and then I'll start lightly on the treadmill. My black belt will have to wait, but I know that won't be the last goal I'm going to have to postpone.

When circumstances arise that are out of your control, you have to learn how to pivot. I think that's where people get into a lot of trouble, because they fall into the trap of not being able to adjust or modify the goal, so they give up. There will never be a direct path from A to B. You're always going to have stuff—a divorce, injury, death of someone you love, even little day-to-day troubles—that can knock you off kilter and pull your focus. There is nothing any of us can do about the obstacles and road-blocks we will inevitably face. What you can control is how you react and how you choose to deal with those challenges. You might take two steps forward one day and then a step back the next, but it's all part of the journey. You just have to keep moving forward. The way I see it, you have three choices when the storm hits. The first is to give up and become a victim. The second is to do what you can to survive. But the third, the one that I set out to do and know we are all capable of, is to learn how to thrive in the storm.

"When you come out of the storm you won't be the same person that walked in. That's what the storm is all about."
—Haruki Murakami